Praise for
Complete Guide to the First Five Years of Marriage,

from which this book is adapted:

"Keeping this book handy can help you build a relationship that stays afloat in spite of money worries, sexual storms . . . and confused communication."

> GARY SMALLEY
> Author, *The DNA of Relationships*

"What happens in the first five years of marriage will largely determine the quality of the marriage for years to come. Here is a book that gives the practical help every couple needs to build a healthy marriage. It should be required reading for all newly married couples."

> GARY D. CHAPMAN, PH.D.
> Author, *The Five Love Languages*
> and *The Four Seasons of Marriage*

"Written by an extraordinary team of counselors . . . filled with practical, biblical advice. You have questions? They have answers! Buy one book for yourself and ten more to use as wedding gifts!"

> CAROL KENT
> Speaker and author of *When I Lay My Isaac Down*

"This new Focus on the Family book is so timely and important for you to read if you're a newly married couple—or to give to that newly married couple in your life. Let this incredible team of marriage and family experts get your marriage off to a great start."

JOHN TRENT, PH.D.
President, The Center for Strong Families
and author of *Breaking the Cycle of Divorce*

"This book is a gem. . . . Packed with wisdom. A perfect gift for any newlywed or engaged couple."

GARY THOMAS
Author, *Sacred Marriage* and *Sacred Influence*

the

SAVVY

Bride's

ANSWER GUIDE

FOCUS ON THE FAMILY®

the SAVVY
BRIDE'S
ANSWER GUIDE

an eye-opening look at your first year of marriage

GENERAL EDITORS
WILFORD WOOTEN, L.M.F.T. & PHILLIP J. SWIHART, PH.D.

 Tyndale House Publishers, Inc., Carol Stream, Illinois

Contents

Introduction 1

1. What Does It Mean to Be a Wife? 5

2. Why Isn't My Husband the Person I Thought He Was? 11

3. Why Isn't My Husband More Like Dad? 15

4. Why Won't He Talk to Me? 21

5. How Can I Get My Husband to Open Up? 27

6. How Can We Talk about Feelings? 31

7. What Does He Want from Our Love Life? 37

8. Why Does My Husband Keep Hurting My Feelings? 43

9. What If I Want Children, but He Doesn't? 49

10. How Well Do I Need to Know My Husband? 55

11. How Honest Do We Have to Be? 61

12. How Can I Get Used to Being Two Instead of One? 67

13. Should I Tell My Husband about My Past? 73

14. How Can I Adjust to My Husband's Personality? 77

15. What Can I Do about His Irritating Habits? 83

16. Why Isn't Marriage the Way I Thought It Would Be? 89

17. How Should We Divide Up the Chores? 93

18. What If My Spouse Won't Take the "Right" Role? 99

19. Do We Have to Have a Budget? 105

20. How Often Is Normal? 111

21. What If We Don't Like the Same Things Sexually? 117

22. Why Don't We Speak the Same Language? 123

23. Is It Okay to Fight? 129

24. How Can We Work Out Disagreements? 135
25. Do I Have to Forgive My Husband? 143
26. How Can I Get Him to Forgive Me? 149
27. How Can Faith Keep Us Together? 155
28. What If an In-law Doesn't Accept Me? 161
29. How Can We Keep from Drifting Apart? 167
30. How Can We Keep the Romance Alive? 171
    Suggested Resources 175
    Notes 177

The Authors

Lon Adams, M.A., L.M.F.T.

Sheryl DeWitt, L.M.F.T., L.M.F.C.C.

James Groesbeck, L.C.S.W., L.M.F.T.

Daniel Huerta, M.S.W., L.C.S.W.

Romie Hurley, L.P.C., N.C.C.

Rob Jackson, M.S., L.P.C., L.M.H.C., N.C.C.

Betty Jordan, R.N., M.A., L.P.C.

Sandra Lundberg, Psy.D.

Glenn Lutjens, M.A., L.M.F.T.

Amy Swierczek

Phillip J. Swihart, Ph.D.

Mitch Temple, M.S., L.M.F.T.

Wilford Wooten, M.S.W., L.M.F.T., L.C.S.W.

ACKNOWLEDGMENTS

We appreciate the monumental editing needed for a volume encompassing the work of so many diverse authors, which was provided by John Duckworth, Senior Book Producer, Focus on the Family. We also wish to recognize our colleague Aarin Hovanec for her perceptive observations and comments. In addition, we're thankful for Sharon Manney's technical assistance in the preparation of this manuscript.

Introduction

When it comes to the Indianapolis 500, it may be difficult to predict which lap will be most critical. But in a marriage, the first five years are central. That's when key adjustments are made and expectations are tested.

How you deal with the large and small crises of your marriage at the start sets important patterns for the future. That's true for brides *and* grooms, no matter whether you tend to run in panic or stay and bury your feelings.

Most marriages start with the delight of "being in love" and honeymoon excitement. The question is what happens next. One spouse put it this way: "I thought the first year would be wonderful. It was hell."

During the first few years, couples "get naked" in more ways than one. And physical nakedness can be much less revealing than many other kinds.

Even in marriages that end up thriving, marital stressors may be—or at least seem to be—more intense in the beginning than later. For instance, it's stressful to find that neither of you seems to have any conflict management skills. As one comedian noted, "My wife and I never fight; we just have moments of intense fellowship."

And then there's sex. Whatever happened to the glorious expectations you had in that wonder-world of dating? It may only take a few months of marital reality for the fantasies of "true love" and sexual excitement to clash with the disappointments of sharing a bed with another imperfect person who's sometimes tough to like, let alone love.

The spiritual dimension of your relationship can be a point of contention early in your marriage, too. These years often form fertile ground for spiritual attack by an enemy who would love to destroy a relationship that God has blessed as holy.

Many of the challenges of the first years stem from distorted expectations. We live in a fast-food culture with a sense of entitlement to having everything happen on demand. But marriage doesn't work that way.

The apostle Paul advised Christians to "work out your salvation with fear and trembling" (Philippians 2:12). As radio Bible teacher Alistair Begg has noted, we need to do the same in our marriages.

This is a book about working things out—trembling or otherwise. In the pages to follow you'll find answers to questions commonly asked by brides and brides-to-be. You'll probably find some issues you're struggling with. It's our hope and prayer that this book will be a rich source of help and encouragement on your journey through the partnership called marriage.

There's another distinctive to this volume, too. The many authors who've contributed have a working relationship with Focus on the Family. Most are professional staff members with Focus on the Family's counseling department. All are committed Christians and highly qualified, licensed mental health, marriage, and family therapists with many years of combined experience in working with thousands of couples and individuals across America.

The early years of marriage are a special adventure. As you

explore your new partnership, explore this book, too. We believe you'll find it to be a thought-provoking source of creative solutions for meeting the challenges of your first years together.

—*Wilford Wooten and Phillip J. Swihart*
General Editors

What Does It Mean to Be a Wife?

Valerie threw her coat to the floor and screamed, "Robert, this is it! I am tired of being treated like a child. You will not allow me to be an adult. You force me to act like a child by the way you treat me. I can't express my opinion or offer any advice. It always has to be your decision—and if I question that decision, you try to argue me back down. I don't know what God intended for a wife to be, but I don't think it was to be like this!"

What *does* it mean to be a wife?

It's a question that's been asked since the beginning of time. Surely every young wife and wife-to-be has at least *thought* about it.

Much of the confusion about what it means to be a wife stems from our culture's messages on the subject. Hollywood often portrays women as independent, strong, superior, and answerable to no one. But is that what a wife should look like? What are her roles? What should a husband expect of her?

If you're struggling with your role (or your spouse's), you're not alone. When these issues are unresolved, it often leads to a sense of hopelessness going into the wedding and a sense of contention afterward.

Let's answer the question by looking at its opposite: What does it *not* mean to be wife? Here are three principles to think about.

1. *A wife is not a maid.* Some husbands expect their wives to take care of all domestic chores. Some wives are content with this arrangement, especially when the husband assumes a handyman role. But both partners should negotiate this and feel comfortable with the result.

Mandy and Maury simplified the division of labor by agreeing that everything inside the home would be her responsibility—and everything outside the door would be his. That worked well until Mandy decided that taking the garbage out, a job she'd been doing, wasn't "inside" work. She voiced her concern to Maury, but it fell on deaf ears. The next day, Maury pulled into the driveway to discover the trash can sitting outside the front door!

Nowhere in Scripture does God command wives, "Thou shalt perform every household task alone, no matter how sick or tired thou mayest become or how many sleepless nights thou hast experienced." God didn't intend a wife to be the family butler, cook, and domestic engineer without support from her husband.

Just as wives are not exempt from helping out with yard work, husbands aren't excused from mutually agreed upon duties inside the home. Was Eve expected to perform every domestic chore by herself? When she became pregnant with Cain, who do you think she depended on? Since no one else was around to help out, we can safely assume that Adam took up the slack.

Adam's view of Eve was reflected in his statement of appreciation when God first presented her to him: "The man said, 'This is now bone of my bones and flesh of my flesh; she shall be called "woman," for she was taken out of man.' For this reason a man will leave his father and mother and be united to his wife, and they will become one flesh" (Genesis 2:23-24). Couples need to adopt the same team approach, recalling that God has brought them together in a partnership.

2. *A wife is not a doormat.* The Bible does say that the husband is the "head" of the wife, and that wives are to be in submission to their husbands. But nowhere does it grant "dictator" status to husbands, or require that wives must fulfill a husband's every wish and command, no matter how unreasonable or uncaring.

Submission is an attitude, a spirit of being under someone's leadership in the domain of marriage. Paul says in Ephesians 5:22, "Wives, submit yourselves to your husbands as to the Lord." But he also says, "Submit to one another out of reverence for Christ" (Ephesians 5:21). Submission doesn't mean that a woman can be mistreated or harmed by her husband simply because he's the leader of the home.

Submission doesn't necessarily mean agreement, either. Just because a wife is under her husband's leadership, she doesn't necessarily agree with everything he does or every decision he makes.

How does that work in real life? Think about what happens when you accept a job. You agree to submit to someone else's authority. You don't give up your freedom and rights as a human being. You're still supposed to be treated with respect and kindness.

Submitting at work is critical to career development. The employee who willingly submits to the job's requirements will get something in return—job satisfaction and the security of regular income. We give, but we also receive.

The same is true of roles in marriage. A wife voluntarily places herself in a position of submission to God and to her husband's leadership. She doesn't give up her individuality. She gives her heart, body, and soul to a relationship of mutuality and service.

If you follow God's commands on how to treat your mate, you'll love, respect, honor, and cherish each other. You'll find no human doormats in your home.

3. *A wife is not to be the downfall of her husband.* God designed women to be husband builders, not husband wreckers. As the Bible puts it, "The LORD God said, 'It is not good for the man to be alone. I will make a helper suitable for him'" (Genesis 2:18).

Adam was engineered to work hard, lead his family, and overcome challenges. God gave Eve the ability, power, and free choice to either build up her husband or tear him down.

Proverbs 14:1 says, "The wise woman builds her house, but with her own hands the foolish one tears hers down." Most wives don't set out to destroy their mates. But they often allow stress, frustration, and resentment to motivate them to treat their husbands in ways that dishonor them. Constant nagging and criticism, for instance, can wear a man down more quickly than a 60-hour week of hard labor! This kind of behavior destroys a man's ability to be what he should be—a confident leader.

When a man feels disrespected and demoralized, he often reacts by withdrawing from the relationship. His ability to be truly close to his wife has a lot to do with how she treats him. As Ephesians 5:33 (AMP) says, "Let the wife see that she respects and reverences her husband—that she notices him, regards him, honors him, prefers him, venerates, and esteems him; and that she defers to him, praises him, and loves and admires him exceedingly."

So what does it mean to be a wife?

There are many ways to answer that question. But here's one

summary you might keep in mind. The apostle Paul urged older women to teach younger women, "so that they will wisely train the young women to be sane and sober-minded—temperate, disciplined—and to love their husbands and their children; to be self-controlled, chaste, homemakers, good-natured (kindhearted), adapting and subordinating themselves to their husbands, that the word of God may not be exposed to reproach—blasphemed or discredited" (Titus 2:4-5, AMP).

—*Mitch Temple*

TAKING IT PERSONALLY

1. How do you think your parents—or others who raised you—would answer the "What does it mean to be a wife?" question? How might their answers have influenced your views on this subject?

2. What appeals to you most about becoming a wife? Try writing a one-page job description that starts with that "duty" and includes at least four other things you'd enjoy.

Why Isn't My Husband the Person I Thought He Was?

2

When she entered counseling with her husband, Erica had one purpose: getting Jim "fixed."

Jim had fallen into patterns that might work for a single guy, but certainly wouldn't do for a married man. He sometimes worked four extra hours without calling to inform Erica, for instance.

He'd changed so much, she thought. When they'd been dating, she'd figured Jim knew how to handle his finances; at least his car was never repossessed. Now they received monthly surprises from MasterCard, detailing Jim's "toy" purchases. Likewise, his apartment had always seemed neat when Erica visited during their courtship. But now his underwear rarely made it the two yards from the foot of their bed to the hamper.

It's easy to understand why Erica hoped the counselor would take on the challenge of setting her husband straight. She wanted the "old" Jim back.

You might be asking yourself these days, "What happened to the guy *I* used to know? Did he change, or was I just seeing him differently then?"

The answer is probably, "Yes." That's because both reflect the truth.

Maybe he *does* act differently now. Your husband probably wanted to seal the deal; he wanted to win your heart. Do you think he would jeopardize losing you by sharing all of his idiosyncrasies with you? Would you do that with him?

Was it deception? It's more like "selective expression." He behaved in a way that he figured would increase your likelihood of saying, "I do." He put his best foot and shiniest shoe forward.

Some of his behavior during those days probably wasn't so deliberate. Thinking of you thrilled his heart during courtship. That type of romantic fire shapes one's actions; loving deeds come easily to one so smitten by romance. You probably felt the same excitement, with your reactions being affected as well.

In Luke 6:32, Jesus conveys this principle with the question, "If you love those who love you, what credit is that to you?" Reciprocating romantic love comes naturally to most people. Over time, it's common for the romance—and therefore some of the motivation for "good behavior"—to fade somewhat.

It's also true that in many ways your husband hasn't changed, but you now view him differently. There are three reasons for that.

1. *Time.* The longer you're married, the more time you have to observe your spouse's behavior. You see things that weren't as noticeable back then.

2. *Distance.* You now see him up close. There's no end to the date, no "See you next week." The artificial nature of dating keeps many behaviors concealed. You currently see him when he's hungry and tired. Women may have their "time of month," but men have their "time of day." When his stomach is empty you may see a whole new side of your man you never knew existed.

3. *Desire.* You viewed your husband during courtship as you

wanted to see him. We tend to construct a person in our minds to match the excitement we want to feel. We mentally create that person in a way that will make us happiest.

So the question becomes, "What do I do now that I've found out he's different from the way I thought he was?"

Debating whether he misrepresented himself or you misread him won't solve anything. Here are three actions you can take.

1. *Choose to love him.* We're told in Ephesians 5:32 that marriage reflects the relationship between Christ and the church. There are inadequacies in the church, yet Christ still loves her.

2. *Look at how you may have changed as well.* Jesus warns in Matthew 7:1-2 that the yardstick we use to judge others will be used to measure us, too.

3. *Realize that you may have legitimate concerns.* Voice them to your husband in a constructive way with the hope that he'll be willing to work toward change—or at least understand your concerns.

Remember Erica? She was surprised when the counselor wasn't willing to "fix" Jim. It wasn't that he didn't recognize the need for changes in Jim's working and spending habits. But the counselor also saw that Erica was mostly trying to control her man.

As Erica worked with the therapist, she saw how she had become less expressive and more withdrawn over time. She began learning ways to communicate her frustrations to Jim in a manner that didn't leave him feeling disrespected.

Erica found that as she and Jim showed more kindness and care toward each other, her feelings toward him deepened. She didn't necessarily feel the same romance as when they courted, but she sensed her love was more mature than it had been before.

—Glenn Lutjens

TAKING IT PERSONALLY

1. If you're a bride-to-be, what change in your husband-to-be would bother you most? If you're already married, what change would you warn your pre-marriage self about if you could?

2. Silently or out loud, practice communicating your frustration to your husband in a way that doesn't leave him feeling disrespected. You could begin by completing this sentence: "When it seems to me that you've become more _____, I feel _____." Then have this conversation when both of you are rested and not pressed for time.

WHY ISN'T MY HUSBAND MORE LIKE DAD?

3

Three little girls were playing in the backyard on the swing. One said, "My dad is the strongest and fastest man in the world."

"No," said the second girl. "My daddy is strongest and fastest!"

"Yeah? Prove it!" the first girl demanded.

"Well, he's faster than a bullet!" the second one boasted.

"That's nothing," the third little girl said. "My daddy can run faster than a car!"

After a short silence, the first girl declared, "My dad is the fastest and I can prove it! He gets off work at five o' clock and is home by four!"

Daughters tend to see their dads as superhuman—or at least special. Research has shown repeatedly that fathers have a huge impact on their girls. For example, close father-daughter relationships foster a sense of competence in girls' mathematical ability. Daughters who live in the same home with and are close to their dads are likely to start dating and having sex at a later age.

Dad is the first man with whom a daughter builds a relationship. That connection forms a framework for the way she views male-female relationships. Dad often teaches her how to make decisions, to work, and to care for others. For better or worse, he teaches her how a husband acts.

No wonder so many wives compare their husbands unfavorably with their dads. But the reality is—and this is big—*your husband is not your father.*

Here are three principles to remember in that regard:

1. *Your husband doesn't have your dad's experience.* When it comes to earning wisdom through practice, your dad has at least 20 years on your husband. Along the way, your father made mistakes and learned from them. So can your husband.

2. *Your dad wasn't perfect.* It's easy to forget someone's imperfections after you've moved away. But there were times when your father let you down, wasn't affectionate, wasn't communicative, wasn't as caring as he needed to be.

3. *Your father and your husband aren't supposed to be the same.* They have two distinct personalities, sets of experiences, families of origin, cultures, and environments in which they were raised. It's impossible for them to be alike. To think otherwise is unfair and unreasonable.

So what do you do? Secretly reprogram your husband to become your dad's twin? Send him to the same company that cloned Dolly the sheep?

No. You have to stop comparing your husband to your father.

If your spouse displays behaviors or attitudes that disturb or hurt you, talk with him about them. Comparisons won't help.

Here are four more suggestions for breaking the comparison habit.

1. *Accent the positives and devalue the negatives.* Parents who harp on the negatives destroy their children's ability to value themselves.

Wives who see in their husbands only the negatives and fail to appreciate the positives destroy their own ability to trust and respect their spouses.

2. *Commit yourself unconditionally to your husband.* "Above all, love each other deeply, because love covers over a multitude of sins" (1 Peter 4:8). Love, respect, and honor your mate in spite of his shortcomings. Allow your commitment to him to inspire you to change the way you see him and his faults.

This doesn't apply, of course, if your husband is abusive or needs help with psychological problems. These conditions need professional assessment and treatment. But annoying habits, mannerisms, and frustrations can be tolerated and dealt with by changes in his behavior or your own attitude.

3. *Honor both your husband and your father.* Your dad deserves your honor and appreciation for his strengths. If you feel he fell short of being a great father, honoring him doesn't mean you approve of his neglect or bad habits. You're not ignoring his failures; you're choosing to honor him for who he is, your father. Taking that attitude, you're likely to work at improving your relationship with him.

The same attitude and approach should be taken with your husband—despite his weaknesses.

4. *Put your husband's faults in perspective.* Mary Andrews, an older lady, was teaching a church class of young, married women. They were discussing problems in marriage when one of the class members raised her hand.

"I realize this appears trivial," the woman said, "but my mom always said that a man who is too lazy to pick up his socks isn't worth a nickel! Well, I married a nickel. My husband never picks up his socks no matter how many times I ask him! He will do it for a day or two; then he goes back to his old habit. It is driving me crazy. I am beginning to lose respect for him."

Other ladies in the class affirmed that they had the same problem with their husbands.

Mary allowed the ladies to vent for a few minutes. Then she said softly, "You know, I had the same problem with my husband." Then she simply looked down and began turning pages in her Bible.

"Well," said a member of the group, "tell us what you did to get him to stop!"

"Actually, I was not successful in getting him to stop throwing his socks on the floor," Mary replied. "We have been married 43 years, and he still does it."

She continued, "I simply decided that this was not the worst habit he could have. My father drank all the time and came home night after night and kept us in constant fear and upheaval. Compared to my father, I came to realize that throwing socks on the floor was a minor battle that I chose not to fight.

"Besides," Mary concluded, "I decided a long time ago: I would rather my husband throw his socks at the foot of my bed than someone else's."

It's okay that your husband is not like your father. Celebrate the differences.

Commitment in marriage means that you've promised your utmost devotion, affection, and unwavering love to an imperfect person. Even if he's nothing like your dad.

—*Mitch Temple*

TAKING IT PERSONALLY

1. If your relationship with your dad were documented in home videos, what would be the highlights?

2. If your father is still living, think of one thing he hasn't quite mastered that your husband (or husband-to-be) is good at. For example, your groom may be able to upgrade an e-mail program for your dad, who can't tell a firewall from a fireplace. Next time you're all together, brag a little about your groom's skill (without putting your father down) and offer his services if he's willing.

WHY WON'T HE TALK TO ME?

A *Non Sequitur* cartoon by Wiley Miller pictures a couple in bed. The wife has put down the book she's been reading and said something to her husband. Here's what he heard: "Time for the annual review of how you make my life a living nightmare."

All she actually said, though, is, "Sweetie, let's talk about us."

Why do some spouses—especially some husbands—seem to view communication as a form of torture?

Betsy is wondering about that. She's hurt that her husband, Carl, seems to have lost interest in her. She interprets his lack of communication as evidence that he doesn't love her. This puts her in a panic; she becomes needy and controlling, trying to force Carl to "talk about the problem." This creates more pressure for Carl, who retreats further.

Carl is overwhelmed by Betsy's need for conversation. It feels like a void that could never be filled. This is decreasing his desire to be intimate with her; he's finding excuses to avoid even spending time together. He'd rather hang out with friends who are less demanding.

When the person you married seems to change into someone else—as Betsy thinks Carl has—it's normal to feel disappointed and even hurt. She knows that part of this change is to be expected after settling into the day-to-day of married life, but she longs for that other guy—the before-marriage one who couldn't seem to stop talking nor get enough of her. She was so excited back then, and believed it would go on forever. Now she feels duped.

Maybe you do, too. Maybe you fear your uncommunicative spouse isn't interested in you, isn't excited about you, or doesn't love you anymore. You might doubt that you married the right person—or feel inadequate, insecure, and desperate for attention.

When that happened to Betsy, she changed, too. Now Carl finds himself wondering what happened to the self-assured, strong woman he first fell in love with. He misses her.

Carl doesn't realize it, but Betsy has always had an unusual need for attention and communication. That's because she had a very stoic father whom she was never able to please. It's good to examine whether your need to talk is reasonable or the result of a troubled upbringing.

Even if the latter is the case, though, most couples need help to discuss their needs in a productive way. Having different attitudes toward talking doesn't mean there is something wrong with either spouse, that anyone was deceived, or that the marriage is hopeless.

Relating to each other is not a technique we're born with. It's like a muscle that needs to be developed over time—and massaged when it hurts.

If you have a spouse who doesn't want to talk as much as you do, the following suggestions may help.

1. *Read about the differences between men and women, especially as they relate to communication.* These differences are a mystery to almost everyone except God, but they may help to explain why your

spouse tends to be the silent type. You could start by reading "Why Don't We Speak the Same Language?" in this book.

2. *Learn to not take things too personally.* In Betsy's case, her need to talk was influenced by her relationship with her father, not just her relationship with Carl.

3. *Don't overanalyze your partner.* Betsy assumed Carl's "lockjaw" was proof that he didn't love her anymore. You may think you know what's behind your spouse's unwillingness to talk, but you can't read his mind.

4. *Talk about your feelings in a non-accusatory, non-blaming way.* To do otherwise will only drive a reluctant talker further away, especially when it comes to discussing emotions.

5. *Ask your spouse what would make him feel less overwhelmed when it comes to communication.* Would it help if you set aside a regular time for talking? If you waited until he decompressed after work?

6. *Ask your spouse for a specific, short commitment of time.* Most reluctant talkers can handle a conversation if they know it won't last forever. Let your mate set the limit. You may find that it increases as he grows more comfortable.

7. *Learn each other's personality type, and how it shapes communication style.* Make the process fun—a discovery of your uniqueness, not an opportunity to stereotype each other.

For more insights on the subject of tight-lipped mates, see "How Can I Get My Husband to Open Up?" in this book.

One of the hardest things for couples to learn is to lay down their lives for each other (see John 15:13) in the mundane world of daily living (see Romans 12:1). Learning to understand the needs of a spouse who talks less or more than you do requires sacrifice. It means not demanding your rights, and loving another as you love yourself. But these are things we can do because God promises to help us by His Holy Spirit if we ask.

It's easy to get discouraged when all you hear from your spouse is silence. It may seem that things are hopeless, but you can gain new perspective through prayer, reading the Bible, or seeking counsel from a pastor or therapist.

Here's what Betsy and Carl did.

Betsy wanted to confess her feelings of hopelessness to Carl about their situation. But she knew she had to do it in a loving and safe environment. One evening she served his favorite meal, then later tucked the children into bed. Then she talked.

His reaction encouraged her. He expressed his support for their marriage and his love for her, which helped her understand that his silence wasn't caused by a lack of caring. Carl revealed how the demands for conversation affected him, and the ways in which he may have been withdrawing for self-protection.

Carl promised to start using a short daily devotional book with Betsy, one she'd bought several months ago and was excited about. The two of them set up a plan for a biweekly date night. They also decided to learn more about healthy communication.

Betsy and Carl recommitted themselves to their marriage. They promised each other that, instead of giving up, they would get help if they needed it.

—Romie Hurley

TAKING IT PERSONALLY

1. If your groom doesn't like to talk, how does he make that clear to you? How do you tend to react? If you think you know his reasons for being silent, how did you reach that conclusion?

2. Betsy took the initiative to express her feelings to Carl in a loving, safe setting. Where and when will an opportunity like that next be available to you? Check your calendar and start planning your conversation.

How Can I Get My Husband to Open Up?

5

Kim opened the pantry door as she began to make dinner. Her heart was heavy and her arms felt weak. Scanning the shelves for something to cook, she felt the familiar, hot sting of tears in her eyes.

She stared at a box of spaghetti. *Why won't Matt talk with me?* she thought. *Doesn't he care how I feel?*

She knew that when her husband came home he'd have an appetite for dinner. But what she hungered for was just a time to talk. *I can open a box of spaghetti, but I can't get Matt to open up,* she thought. *He never tells me what he's thinking or feeling.*

Sighing, she reached out for a jar of sauce. *How will we ever get to know each other at this rate? We've been married for almost two years, and I don't understand him any better than I did before our honeymoon.*

She took a heavy pot to the sink and began to fill it with cold water. *I've got to get a grip,* she thought, shaking her head. *It's not like our marriage is on the rocks. We're faithful to each other. He doesn't put me down or blame me when things get screwed up.*

Suddenly she had an idea. *Meatballs! I'll make Matt his favorite homemade garlic meatballs. He's sure to notice. And while we're eating dinner, maybe he'll finally open up.*

The strength in her arms started to return. She flew through the kitchen. Soon the atmosphere was inviting and warm. She even lit a candle for the table.

When Matt came home, he kissed Kim and they sat down to eat. Kim launched into an animated account of her day, assuming her excitement would show Matt what she wanted—conversation. But Matt was his usual quiet self. He didn't seem to notice the meatballs. He silently chewed and nodded.

Okay, she thought as they began to clear the table. *I shouldn't expect him to read my mind. I'll just come right out and tell him what I want.*

She started talking, explaining as clearly as she could how much she needed him to open up.

Unfortunately, all Matt heard was criticism. He shot back that he already did so much for her. He worked long hours and provided well for them. They even prayed together. What more could she expect?

The evening ended on a sour note. They both knew they had a problem, and needed help.

They called their pastor, who quickly referred them to a counselor in their church. As Kim and Matt told the counselor their stories, it became clear that Kim was having difficulty accepting the fact that Matt showed his love for her primarily through action—working hard—rather than by talking with her. As Matt listened to Kim, he began to realize that his actions weren't enough; they had to be accompanied by loving words that would speak to Kim's heart.

After considering the couple's situation, the counselor suggested a way to get conversation flowing between them. He called it "the Ten-Minute Plan."

Here's how it worked. The goal was to help Kim and Matt connect—in a way that fit their busy schedules. Three times a week, they were to spend four minutes reading a recommended marriage book together, four minutes having a positive discussion (no criticism), and two minutes praying. That was it—ten minutes of affirmation through reading, talking, listening, and praying, three times weekly.

It sounded easier than it turned out to be. But Kim and Matt didn't give up. They knew their marriage was at a turning point, and this crisis was an opportunity to enrich their lives together. They were determined that with God, good counseling, and a plan of action, they would make their good marriage great.

The Ten-Minute Plan worked so well that they soon wanted more interaction—and more minutes together. They set aside time each week to do a routine task, giving them a comfortable context in which to talk even more.

The task was to prepare one meal together. They'd plan the menu on Wednesdays, shop on Thursdays, and cook on Fridays. At first their meals were very American, but exploring cookbooks led them to discover international cuisine. That caused their interest in other countries to soar.

That interest, in turn, led to curiosity about missions and missionaries. As Kim and Matt prepared food from other cultures, they prayed for missionaries and discussed ways to support them.

By talking and listening, Kim and Matt found themselves more willing to open up to each other and adapt to each other's needs. They set aside even more time for loving talk and listening. Soon they knew each other better than ever.

As you try to get to know your spouse, is it hard for him to open up? Here are five principles to remember:

1. Communicate your need for conversation in a clear, respectful, forthright way; don't assume your spouse knows what you're thinking.

2. Notice when your spouse *does* try to talk with you. Express your appreciation for that with sincerity and kindness.

3. Commit yourselves to the Ten-Minute Plan of reading, talking, listening, and praying together. Don't give up even though it may be difficult at first.

4. Turn a routine activity into a time of conversation. For Kim and Matt it was cooking; for you and your spouse it could be anything from shopping to hiking to visiting garage sales.

5. Maintain a sense of humor about unexpected challenges in your conversations. Be patient and persistent.

As Kim and Matt found, it *is* possible to help a spouse open up. If it doesn't happen for you as quickly as it happened for them, keep at it!

—*James Groesbeck with Amy Swierczek*

Taking It Personally

1. Have you ever felt like Kim? What did you do? What was the result?

2. Try the Ten-Minute Plan this week. Then choose a routine activity (doing the dishes, grocery shopping, walking the dog) during which you can talk without pressure. Finally, give your groom a thank-you note next time he makes an effort to communicate positively with you.

How Can We Talk
about Feelings?

6

You were designed to have emotions and to validate your spouse's emotions. It was God's idea.

You need to talk about those emotions. But how can you do that without creating conflict?

Janeen wants to talk about feelings. She's having trouble with a coworker. Her husband Jerry is willing to listen for a while to her story, but then he proceeds to tell Janeen what she should do. For Jerry the subject is completed, closed; the problem is solved.

But Janeen doesn't want a problem-solving session. She only desires to be heard. She needs Jerry to be a safe sounding board, and she doesn't want this used against her later.

Even though this "feelings discussion" didn't begin with an issue between Janeen and Jerry, it ends there. Janeen's response is resentment and bitterness. Next time she needs to talk about feelings, she may not confide in him.

A week later Jerry has a disagreement with his father. Janeen, wanting to be helpful, follows Jerry around and tries to get him to talk about his feelings. But Jerry needs to be by himself to give this situation some thought.

"Just leave me alone!" Jerry finally yells.

Jerry, like most men, needs space to work through problems. Not understanding this, Janeen triggers an argument. Next time Jerry may not reveal his pain to her, either.

Talking about your feelings is an art. Whether you're more like Janeen or Jerry, you want a partner who honors you by listening when you're ready. You want your spouse to acknowledge your pain, to hear the options you've formulated, to give you equal status. If these things don't happen, the relationship doesn't feel safe. The depth of the conversation becomes shallow and unsatisfying.

Intimacy in a marriage begins when each spouse takes responsibility for his or her emotions and behaviors. This is more likely to happen in a climate free from judgment, defensiveness, and blame.

When Janeen reports problems with a coworker and Jerry responds as problem solver, she can use "straight talk" with Jerry. For example: "When I'm not allowed to finish my sentences, I feel discounted and unimportant to you. What I need is to be heard."

When Jerry takes responsibility for the hurt he feels because of his father's comments, Janeen can promote intimacy by listening. She can draw him out to express what he's ready to say. Only when Jerry feels safe will he disclose to Janeen his deepest feelings and any related history. Their closeness will be enhanced.

When you have feelings you'd like to express, it may be helpful to pray or journal about them first. Tell your heavenly Father how you're feeling before you address the issue with your mate. You can find comfort in looking to Him first.

What should you do when the feelings you want to talk about

are likely to spark an argument? Once you've taken responsibility for how you feel, then conflict resolution can begin. A good place to start is by clarifying the issue, saying something like, "Is this what you meant?" Many arguments are about misunderstanding the actual issue.

For instance, let's say that Jerry tells Janeen, "We're really short on money this month."

Janeen responds defensively by saying, "It isn't my fault!"

It would have been better for her to get Jerry's clarification of the money situation. "What are you trying to tell me?" she could have asked.

That doesn't mean she'll agree with his answer. Clarifying simply enables you to understand your spouse's perspective. This honors your mate and allows both of you to start at the same place.

Talking about feelings is challenging enough in itself, but other factors can make it harder. First, there's the "child challenge." If you have kids, they're probably clamoring for attention often—even when the two of you need time and quiet to talk about emotions. Janeen and Jerry, who have eight-month-old twin boys, need to develop intimacy skills and schedule time to address feelings. If this doesn't occur, the emotions won't go away; someone else (coworker, friend, relative) will be selected as a confidant. A wedge may be driven between Jerry and Janeen, and counseling may be needed to repair the damage.

Then there's the "childhood challenge." Sometimes a person enters a marriage without having been nurtured as a child. Missy, for example, had a mother who was an alcoholic. Never experiencing unconditional love, Missy became the "parent" at age three. When her husband, William, attempts to nurture her now by talking about feelings—even positive ones like love, joy, and peace—it feels foreign and uncomfortable to her. Missy and William may need counseling to address this unfinished business, so she can express feelings and receive nurturing.

So how can you talk about feelings?

- By being respectful and honoring when your spouse takes responsibility for his emotions and behaviors;
- By understanding how the communication styles of men and women differ;
- By developing conflict resolution strategies;
- By intentionally nurturing one another;
- By committing yourself to make this an enjoyable marriage; and
- By keeping a prayer journal to release frustration.

This sets the stage for safe self-disclosure. What happens next is up to you.

—Betty Jordan

Taking It Personally

1. Which of the following seems to be the biggest obstacle to talking with your husband (or husband-to-be) about feelings: gender differences, the "child challenge," or the "childhood challenge"? Why?

2. If you tend to "hound" your partner to discuss feelings, practice listening to him instead. Let him choose the topic. Listen especially for any emotion he expresses, even inadvertently— enthusiasm for a favorite TV show, for instance, or disgust for a crooked politician. Acknowledge the feelings without criticizing them. This can be a small but significant step toward creating a safe place to discuss deeper emotions.

What Does He Want from Our Love Life?

7

Julie watched the attractive, career-oriented women at her husband's office party and felt an unfamiliar pang of worry.

Derek was naturally outgoing, and that ability to connect with others had been a big factor in his success in sales. A devoted Christian, he'd never given her reason to doubt his fidelity. But it was obvious women noticed him.

What was it the expert on that talk show had said? "If you don't romance your husband, someone else will."

Julie shivered. Their sex life had been declining since their honeymoon three years earlier. She'd never really understood what had gone wrong.

What does he want from me? she thought.

Do you ever wonder the same thing about your husband? Magazine articles at the supermarket checkout counter may feature articles about "Twelve Secret Ways to Please Your Man," but does your spouse really want you to show up at the front door in Saran Wrap?

Like most other aspects of marriage, it's not that simple.

Women are often characterized as mysterious and men as more basic and straightforward. But one-dimensional stereotypes about sports cars versus pickup trucks only take us so far. Men can be inscrutable, too—and a wife who wants to be a good sexual partner looks for keys to unlock his mysteries as well.

Here are five steps toward being the partner your husband wants.

1. *Be secure in your own sexuality.* Be proactive. Instead of maintaining a passive role, invest in the growth and development of your sex life. Rather than leaving him to guess your needs and preferences, speak candidly and without criticizing. Especially if your husband was sexually pure before marriage, there are things that only you can teach him about what you want.

Many husbands wish their wives would more often initiate sex. In the safety of this God-ordained arena, they want to be pursued. The feeling that he's desirable meets a deep need in every man. Find out how he likes to be approached and add that to the menu occasionally.

2. *Affirm his masculinity.* There are non-sexual ways to affirm your husband, too. In private, you either build or diminish his confidence in the way you regard his interests, hobbies, parenting skills, and friendships. Showing respect for the things that are important to him directly affects your whole relationship.

There are opportunities to affirm your husband in public as well. Consider how you talk to others about him, especially in his presence. Criticism or barbed jests quickly shoot down intimacy on every level, physical or otherwise. And even though nonsexual touch is often described as a woman's need, your hand on his hand or shoulder tells him and others, "This man is mine, and I'm glad."

3. *Give him freedom of access.* It's a thorny subject, but a husband's feeling of having to "beg" for sex is too common a complaint to omit. While you aren't supposed to be some kind of 24-hour convenience mart, do examine your attitude of availability. If you find

yourself frequently making excuses, figure out what's behind that pattern. Do your part to identify and eliminate the barriers that keep you from enjoying sex, so you can be a receptive, enthusiastic partner.

Part of receptivity includes keeping him informed of your menstrual period, ovulation, premenstrual syndrome (PMS), and other physical needs or limitations. The intricate, delicate nature of a woman's body bewilders and intimidates many husbands. Take the time to demystify your gynecological or obstetric issues. This will allow him to be a more confident partner while building intimacy in your marriage.

When physical or other issues prohibit intercourse, explain why—assuring your husband that you aren't just putting him off indefinitely. Be aware that even when your libido is low, his may be as strong as ever. Use creativity and teamwork to find a menu of sexual touch that will satisfy both partners' needs until intercourse is possible again.

4. *Understand his sexual needs.* Men need sex in order to feel intimate; women need intimacy in order to feel sexual. While this is a broad generalization, it describes a basic contrast in our creation. Testosterone causes your husband to desire and think about sex more than you do. Most men desire sex at least three times a week and think of it more often than that.

While you shouldn't blindly force yourself to serve him sexually whether you feel like it or not, at least start by asking him what his needs are. Your discussion should assure him that you don't see your differences as an issue of bad versus good. It's important for him to know you understand his needs and that you care about meeting them.

5. *Help him stay faithful.* A man's visually-oriented arousal mechanism is part of God's purposeful design. The fact that your husband delights in how you look, feel, and smell can be a source of enjoyment for you both. Neither of you should obsess over appearance or compare yourself to Hollywood icons, but general attention to how you keep yourself is an important part of his sensory experience.

Be especially mindful of how our culture affects men. Pray for your husband's spiritual, emotional, and physical protection. Provide a safe environment in which he can admit his inevitable struggles and temptations. Don't enable him with a "boys will be boys" attitude, but don't judge him for being tempted, either. Rather, consider his vulnerability a sacred trust that can bond you closer as you serve each other in Christ.

Driving home from the office party, Julie took a deep breath. "Derek," she said finally, "I want to make sure I'm meeting your needs as a wife."

Derek's eyes widened. "You mean . . . um . . . sexually?"

"Well, yeah. Those women obviously noticed you. I just want to make sure you feel . . . satisfied."

Derek looked thoughtful. After a long moment he reached over and gently squeezed her hand. "That's really nice of you to say. I know we have some things to work on, but I'm very satisfied with you. I thought you knew that."

Julie sighed. "Sometimes I don't understand what I should do. I want to be the kind of wife you can talk to. I mean, to tell me if there are things you wish were different or better. We need to talk more."

Derek nodded slowly.

We might not be there yet, Julie thought. *But it's a start.*

—*Rob Jackson*

Taking It Personally

1. Where have you tended to collect information about the role sex plays in a man's life? From Hollywood? Past relationships? The gossip of girlfriends? Do these assumptions make you feel more confident about the sexual aspect of your marriage, or less? Why?

2. Read *The Way to Love Your Wife* by Clifford and Joyce Penner (Tyndale/Focus on the Family, 2007). This book, designed to help men meet their wives' sexual needs, will give you new insights into your husband's desires, temptations, and insecurities, too.

Why Does My Husband
Keep Hurting My Feelings?

8

Does your spouse ever claim to be teasing when you think he's really just being cruel?

Do you ever feel his nagging about your weight stems from insensitivity, not concern for your health?

Ever wonder whether his habit of pointing out your flaws in public has more to do with his mean streak than with the part of the country he's from?

Many couples suffer from a perpetual case of individual or mutual heartlessness. Maybe you've seen an example in the ever-bickering Frank and Marie Barone on reruns of TV's *Everybody Loves Raymond*. Marie makes a brainless observation; Frank counters with a cutting remark. Marie comes back with a crude nickname. The pattern continues from one scene to the next.

The Bible instructs us repeatedly to treat each other with kindness, honor, and respect. These commands were designed to be applied to any relationship, especially marriage. As sacred as marriage is to God, you can rest assured that it displeases Him to see husbands and wives haphazardly wounding each other's spirits with potshots like these:

- "Can't you do anything right?"
- "You always make dumb choices like this!"
- "You act like your mother."
- "You are such a baby. Everything I say hurts your feelings."
- "How many times do I have to tell you to mow the lawn? Are you deaf or do you just not care?"
- "Can't you see I'm watching this show? Just let me unwind for a few minutes!"

If you look long enough, you'll find a counselor who'll label this kind of behavior with a diagnosis. But the simple fact is that some couples, like Frank and Marie Barone, are just plain cruel and have adopted uncaring spirits.

In many cases, though, ongoing patterns of hurt feelings can stem from two possible sources: a hypersensitive spouse or an insensitive one.

Being overly sensitive can be just as destructive as its opposite. If you take offense at every perceived slight, your spouse probably will walk around on eggshells, trying not to upset you. He will run everything through the "Will this hurt her feelings?" filter. People who live with hypersensitive mates often respond by withdrawing, becoming resentful, or being terrified to say or do anything.

Hypersensitivity is common in people who allow what they feel to become the primary factor in determining how they see themselves and others, and how they respond to criticism and perceived threats. It can be a precursor to deeper, more destructive emotional and relational problems. It also can be a symptom of Avoidant Personality Disorder, a condition marked by timidity, low self-esteem, and excessive sensitivity to rejection. If you or your spouse fits the criteria for this disorder, professional intervention is needed.

The opposite of being too sensitive is insensitivity, which can be just as debilitating. An insensitive person "throws" his thoughts, words, and behaviors out there and lets the chips fall where they may. He may experience a temporary feeling of freedom by "getting it out on the table," but doesn't realize the price of his liberation may be revolutionary war.

Insensitive people are habitual violators of the command to "be kind and compassionate to one another, forgiving each other, just as in Christ God forgave you" (Ephesians 4:32). Insensitivity sometimes indicates a serious personality disorder called narcissism. People with this problem are excessively self-centered, lacking concern or empathy for others. Often they're unable to recognize when they've hurt another's feelings, and don't control their hurtful behaviors without professional help.

Apart from personality disorders, if you or your mate has allowed insensitivity or hypersensitivity to set up camp in your marriage, beware that it can destroy your relationship if left unattended. Changes in attitude, behavior, and spiritual direction—including genuine remorse and repentance—are necessary.

If this is the case in your marriage, here are some practical steps to take.

1. *Educate yourself about the problem, whether it's yours or your spouse's.* Knowledge often leads to understanding, which often leads to resolution.

Melanie felt verbally abused by her husband, Larry. She decided to learn as much as possible about this problem and how others have dealt with it. Through sources on the Internet she discovered that one of the first steps in dealing with verbally abusive spouses is to understand what drives the abuse.

After several weeks of reading and seeking advice from people she trusted, Melanie realized that some of Larry's behavior stemmed from being raised by a physically abusive father. She began to respond with less resentment to Larry's hurtful words. As her responses became less threatening to Larry, the intensity of his verbal attacks lessened. A dialogue opened up between the two. Eventually this led to professional counseling.

2. *Make your concerns known to your spouse in a nonthreatening way.* Don't use accusatory language like, "It's your problem, not mine," or "You are just too insensitive." Describe how you feel when your mate uses hurtful words. Describe how long the hurt lasts and how it may possibly lead to inappropriate responses on your part—like ongoing resentment or withdrawal.

3. *Be transparent about your own sensitivity or insensitivity.* Often your willingness to admit a weakness will encourage your spouse to acknowledge his own flaws.

4. *Realize that God will judge us according to the way we treat others.* He doesn't approve of willful, malicious, hurtful actions. Jesus said, "But I tell you that men will have to give account on the day of judgment for every careless word they have spoken" (Matthew 12:36). Couples are not exempt from this warning.

5. *Consider whether insensitivity has escalated into abuse.* Any words can become abusive when they're intended to hurt someone else. God calls this malicious and forbids it (1 Timothy 3:11).

James described the tongue as being "full of deadly poison" (3:8). David said in Psalm 52:2 that the tongue is like a "sharpened razor" that works to bring about the destruction of others. Proverbs 12:18 states that "reckless words pierce like a sword."

6. *Seek professional help.* If this is an ongoing problem, locate a Christian psychologist or psychiatrist who can assess and treat personality disorders. Even if your spouse doesn't want to participate, a professional therapist often can offer direction on how to live with someone who has verbally abusive tendencies and how to manage the situation.

Abusive words can cause so much pain that neither you nor your spouse can be objective enough to develop solutions. That's where a counselor can help. If abusive language turns into physical abuse, seek shelter and professional assistance immediately.

7. *Pray for your spouse.* Prayer can change situations and people, even if nothing else can. Jesus told us to pray for those who hurt us (Matthew 5:44). If He commands us to pray for our enemies, surely He expects us to pray for an insensitive spouse.

Hurtful emotions have a way of overshadowing the need to do what's right. Jesus tells us to pray for people like these, even if we don't feel like it. Maybe He did that not just for the benefit of those whose words hurt us, but for ourselves as well.

—*Mitch Temple*

Taking It Personally

1. Would your husband (or fiancé) say that you're oversensitive? How do you know you aren't?

2. Which of the following steps have you taken already? Which will you take this week? (a) Educating yourself about the problem; (b) making your concerns known to your spouse in a nonthreatening way; (c) being transparent about your own sensitivity or insensitivity; (d) realizing that God will judge us according to the way we treat others; (e) considering whether insensitivity has escalated into abuse; (f) seeking professional help; (g) praying for your spouse.

What If I Want Children, but He Doesn't?

9

Todd and Amanda were having *that* argument—again.

"I'm just not sure I'm ready to be a father!" Todd protested. "And I don't know if I can provide for a family."

"Todd, there's never going to be a perfect time for us to have kids. We need to look at starting our family now."

"We've always talked about you staying home if we have kids," Todd said. "We're spending more than we're making with *both* of us working. I just don't see how we can do it."

"Well, let's take another look at the budget and see what we can cut," Amanda countered. "We can try living on just your income for a few months and saving mine."

"We tried that. We couldn't pull it off."

"But this time I'm really committed."

Todd tried a different approach. "Well, what about the kind of parents we'd be? I mean, we don't want me to be like my dad."

"You're not like your dad."

"I might turn out to be."

And so it went—again.

Todd and Amanda may not be handling their conflict very well, but they're asking some important questions. When one spouse wants to start a family and the other doesn't, it's vital to work through that disagreement and find a way to proceed that's comfortable for both of you.

How do you work it through? Here are some suggestions.

1. *Realize that men and women approach this issue differently.* Many wives talk about the "ticking" of their "biological clock." This has different meanings for different women. Some are describing their longing for a cuddly infant, a longing they feel every time they see a baby and are reminded of the fact that they're not pregnant. Other women are concerned about their age and fertility.

Husbands, meanwhile, tend to have other concerns. They may be reluctant to have children because they're worried about providing for the family financially—or about what kind of fathers they'll be.

That's not to say men are always the reluctant ones. A wife might be concerned about finances or about how she'd care for the baby. She may fear the death of her career, or the possibility that her free-dom to stay home with the baby will be a huge strain on her hus-band, or that her body won't stand up to the changes and stresses of pregnancy.

2. *Remember that "not now" doesn't always mean "never."* There's a big difference between wanting to have a baby and wanting to have a baby *now*. This may not be the best time; it certainly isn't if your spouse isn't comfortable with it.

If you're concerned that waiting may cause problems with fertil-ity due to your age, talk with your physician—and then with your spouse. It's better to approach your mate with information, not just emotion.

3. *Don't pressure your spouse.* Avoid placing undue pressure on an uncertain partner. To assert, "If you loved me, you'd change your

mind," is a sophomoric argument. This is a lifelong commitment for both of you; playing emotional games over the creation of a new life is not the answer.

Pressure can actually make the problem worse. A spouse may say, "No, I don't want kids," in order to avoid further prodding and questions he can't answer.

4. *Don't deceive your spouse.* Respect each other and seek honest agreement. Do *not* surprise your spouse with a pregnancy by sabotaging the contraceptives. Parenting is far too important for deceptive behavior to be part of it.

If having children continues to be your desire, keep praying and talking about it. Given time, your spouse may have a change of heart. Instead of manipulating, trust God for the outcome.

5. *Act on accurate information.* Some reluctant spouses are worried about passing on a genetic problem. If this is the case with yours, both of you should meet with a specialist. Ask your doctor to refer you. The specialist can evaluate your families' medical histories and often can test to determine the likelihood of passing on a disorder. Then you can make a prayerful decision based on the most complete information available.

Be aware, however, that any genetic counseling you receive will have a margin of error. Ask the specialist about rates of false positive and false negative test results. We can plan and predict, but we can't control. Only God can do that.

6. *Aim patiently for consensus.* A "no" right now is not necessarily permanent. But it may take time to get to "yes."

Consider this analogy. Let's say you want to have sex tonight and your spouse doesn't. If he says, "Not right now, Honey, I'm really tired and stressed," would it be a good idea to say, "It's now or never"?

With patience, you soon may find your spouse taking you up on your offer. You may have to bring it up when he's more receptive. Or the two of you might set a date in the not-too-distant future.

So it is with starting a family. You don't want to coerce your spouse into having a child; you want him to be an eager participant. If you're not jointly committed to this, you need to wait.

In the case of Todd and Amanda, they kept talking about becoming parents. They agreed that Todd's biggest reservations centered around finances and being a poor role model. So they took action in both areas.

On the financial front, they decided that for one year they'd live on Todd's income and save Amanda's. They put her pay in a separate account so they'd be less tempted to spend it.

During that year they also read four books on becoming parents and developed friendships with two couples who had children. Todd and Amanda babysat for the other couples and saw how exhausting—and what a joy—it can be to care for little ones.

By the end of the year Amanda and Todd felt much better prepared to have children themselves. They didn't have *that* argument anymore. And even Todd looked forward to parenting as the next stage of their lives.

—Sandra Lundberg

TAKING IT PERSONALLY

1. Why do you suppose you feel more urgency about having children than your spouse does? Is his reluctance mostly about preparedness, finances, freedom, or something else?

2. What four books could you and your husband read in order to feel better prepared for parenthood? What couple could you spend time with, observing the everyday realities of parenting? How much money could you set aside in a year to cushion the shock of starting a family? Which of these steps would help you most?

How Well Do I Need to Know My Husband?

10

When it comes to creating closeness in marriage, honesty is essential. But should you and your spouse know everything about each other?

What if you don't like what your spouse has to say about his past? And if there are secrets between you, will that lead to mistrust, doubt—even divorce?

When the two of you are vulnerable and transparent, it helps each of you understand where the other is coming from—which cultivates patience and compassion. But sometimes "letting it all hang out" can hurt a relationship. Where should you draw the line?

To help you know what kinds of information are really necessary, here are nine questions you *do* need to ask your spouse.

1. *"How were you raised?"*

There's no greater influence on your spouse than the way he grew up. Ask: "How did you get along with your mother and father? Were your growing-up years pleasant? Hurtful? What did you like about the way you were raised? What didn't you like? How do you think childhood may have shaped your views of the opposite sex, yourself, and intimacy (emotional and physical)? Have you dealt with any pain from the past? If so, how? If not, are you planning to do so?"

One wife discovered how valuable this kind of conversation can be. "Understanding that Brett and his mother didn't get along gave me some insight into our relationship," she said. "Brett's mother always criticized him and made him feel worthless. If he didn't please her, she would withdraw for days to punish him. Learning how his mom approached him and prefacing my confrontation by telling him I love him and I am not going anywhere but that I just want to resolve our issue, has helped a lot. Before I understood his fear of me abandoning him like his mom did, whenever I confronted him he would internalize everything so as not to upset me for fear I would leave. This never accomplished anything. Now he's willing to speak his mind with me."

Understanding your spouse in this way helps you not to take it personally when old patterns cause problems. It also helps you work together to overcome them.

2. *"How would you describe your relationship with God?"*

For Christians, marriage is a total commitment of two people to the Lord and to each other. It's a partnership intended to allow spouses to be themselves fully, to help refine each other, and to encourage each other to become the people God created them to be. For this union to be as successful as the Lord designed it to be, you need to understand how much you and your partner have in common when it comes to faith.

3. *"How do you deal with finances?"*

Tammy complained to her sister, "Larry grew up in a family where his mother took care of all the finances. She paid the bills and decided how the money was to be spent. I'm not good with finances and don't want that responsibility. I assumed that the man was responsible for the budget in the household."

Larry and Tammy needed to discuss how money was to be handled in their house. Both had come into marriage with different expectations but hadn't talked about them.

When they finally sat down and discussed finances, they decided Larry would be in charge of paying the bills because he seemed to have been gifted with financial wisdom. They mapped out a budget, and pledged that before any big purchases were made, they'd agree on them together.

4. *"How do you see the roles of husband and wife?"*

"My mom was a stay-at-home mother," Quinn said. "She took care of the house and the kids. When Kathy went back to work, we would fight all the time because she didn't take care of the house like she should."

Kathy saw things differently: "Our finances were tight, so I wanted to go back to work. But he still expects that I cook, clean, and do all the caretaking of the house. He believes that's the woman's job. I think we should share the chores because we're both working. His view of our roles is much more traditional than how I feel is best for the both of us."

It's important to find out how your spouse thinks husband-wife roles should play out in your household, and how those roles might change during the seasons of your marriage. In the case of Quinn and Kathy, they decided that while she worked they would share chores—but when she was able to stay home, Quinn would be the breadwinner and Kathy would be in charge of household upkeep.

5. *"What roles should in-laws have?"*

What part does your spouse see both sets of parents playing in your life together?

"Susan always seeks her dad's advice before she seeks mine," Caleb says. "I love her dad, but feel it's my role as her husband to have her talk things over with me first." Having been pretty independent from an early age, Caleb feels betrayed and not trusted by Susan when she involves her parents in every decision.

Melina, on the other hand, grew up without a mom. She's come to love her husband, Spencer's, mother as if she were her own, and consults her mother-in-law on many decisions. Because Spencer is so close to his folks and trusts them implicitly, he enjoys the fact that Melina is willing to seek their counsel.

The way you deal with in-laws will depend on the depth and type of relationship you have with them. Make sure you understand your spouse's view of that relationship and what that means practically.

6. *"What do you expect regarding our sexual relationship?"*

Does your spouse believe sex is for procreation, relaxation, pleasure and fun, expressing intimacy, or all of the above?

Ask: "What kinds of things stimulate you? Who do you want to be the initiator? How would you like me to suggest having sex? How should I tell you I'm not in the mood? How often do you think we should have sex?"

One wife, Mary Lee, said, "I always heard that the man was to be the initiator in sex. But when I asked Jim what he thought about that, he told me it would please him if I took initiative at times. It would make him feel like I desired him rather than just feeling like I was only accommodating his desires." The two of them discovered how freeing it was to talk about these things instead of having unspoken—and unmet—expectations.

7. *"What are your goals—for yourself and for us?"*

Ask your spouse what his or her dreams are. "Kevin is an incredible businessman," one wife said. "He's always been very diligent to work hard and provide well for our family. I thought he was happy until I asked him what he would do if he could do anything in the world. He said he would be in the ministry. He's now going to seminary. I'm so happy I asked him his dream; otherwise he may have stayed stuck in a job that supported us but wasn't fulfilling to him."

Helping your partner pursue his passions is vital to your marriage's health. You won't know those dreams if you don't ask.

Inquire about your spouse's goal for your marriage, too. Is it closeness? Wealth? To have a family? Career success? To be used as a team in some ministry? Discuss these dreams and set realistic goals with time limits. For example: "In five years we want to be out of debt." "In one year we want to save enough money to go on a family mission trip."

8. *"How did you communicate and resolve conflict in your family?"*

In tears, Elizabeth told her mother, "Bobby yells at me when we talk to each other." Elizabeth didn't understand how her husband could think that was okay. She was an only child who'd rarely had conflicts with her family.

Bobby, on the other hand, was the youngest of five brothers. His was a fun-loving family that spoke loudly and often. He thought he was just talking passionately to Elizabeth; she heard it as yelling.

When the two of them finally discussed their families' communication styles, they began to understand the differences. Elizabeth no longer felt "run over," while Bobby saw that his wife's low-intensity way of talking didn't mean that she was indifferent.

9. *"Are there medical issues in your family?"*

Do heart disease, diabetes, or other medical problems run in your mate's family? Is your spouse dealing with a chronic condition? How is it treated? Have there been unusual deaths in the family?

It's important to know your spouse's medical history so that you can work together to prevent further problems, collaborate on diet and exercise, and consider possible implications for your children.

As you ask these nine questions, keep your spouse's temperament in mind. If he seems hesitant to talk, don't nag. Just explain why you're looking for information and how it can bring you closer.

Remember the importance of timing, too. For example, if your mate ignored your interest in sexual intimacy last night, try waiting until neither of you is upset to discuss sexual expectations. Likewise, a spouse who's tired, stressed, or sick won't be able to focus on the issues. As for a mate who's asked about family history, he may need time to gather information—or just think.

Be considerate of your spouse's feelings. But don't neglect to ask these questions. The only way to understand your mate is to know him.

—*Sheryl DeWitt*

Taking It Personally

1. Which of the nine questions are you most interested in asking? Why? Are there any questions you're reluctant to ask because you might not like the answer? If so, would it help to promise each other that the two of you will talk with a pastor or counselor if the discussion leads to conflict?

2. Rather than dumping all nine questions on your husband (or husband-to-be) at once, plan to discuss one each week for the next nine weeks. Set a time that works for both of you. Ask each other the question of the week; it shouldn't be a one-way interrogation.

How Honest Do We Have to Be?

11

1. Healthy relationships are built on trust.

2. If you aren't totally honest, trust is impossible.

3. Without trust, the relationship crumbles.

This sounds simple—too simple, as it turns out.

If you're a Christian, are you required to be "absolutely" honest with your spouse? After all, the Scriptures are clear that lying is a serious affront to God. Christians are to strive for honesty—and truth is absolute, not relative.

But what does that mean when you ask, "Does this dress make me look fat?" What does it mean when your husband was intimate with a girlfriend before he met you?

In other words, does perfect honesty exist in imperfect human relationships? And if you aren't completely candid with your spouse, will your marriage fall apart?

To answer those questions, we need to ask another: What does "honest" mean?

To be honest certainly is to tell the truth. But by "honest" do you mean simply that whatever you communicate is accurate? Or do you also mean that you're obligated to communicate all information on any and all topics, both from your present and past?

Being honest in the sense of telling the truth is not the same as imparting every thought and feeling you have. Joe and Suzie learned that the hard way.

They'd been married two years. Suzie often remembered that Joe had been "honest" in telling her during a premarital counseling session that he'd had sexual experiences with two other women before becoming a Christian five years ago. He'd also told her that no children had been the result of these liaisons, and that he'd never contracted any sexually transmitted diseases.

Suzie came into the marriage a virgin, but didn't think Joe's sexual history would be a problem for her. As time went by, however, she found herself thinking more and more about these "other women" and Joe's experiences with them. She decided to be "honest" and tell her husband that she was increasingly anxious about his past dalliances. If he would just answer a couple of questions, she said, she'd be able to forget the whole thing.

Wanting to put her concern to rest, Joe reluctantly agreed to talk briefly about these old girlfriends. Suzie wanted to know their names, how they looked, why Joe was attracted to them, how long he dated them, and whether he was in love with them at the time.

He was "honest" in describing one of them as a cute, sexy blonde and the other as an attractive, more intellectual redhead. He recalled being fascinated with the redhead, and "falling in love" or at least "in lust" with the blonde. Neither relationship lasted long after a brief sexual affair.

Much to Joe's disappointment, these "honest" answers did nothing to satisfy Suzie's increasing obsession with his history. She seemed even more anxious and began to demand detailed, intimate information about the two sexual relationships. Joe began to withdraw from

Suzie's "interrogations" as he called them, and refused to talk with her about anything in his past.

Suzie, meanwhile, began to accuse Joe of hiding things from her. She said she could no longer trust him.

For Joe and Suzie, this effort to be "honest" turned into a painful, ugly series of interchanges that became toxic for their relationship, the dynamics of which remained unclear to both of them.

So is honesty the best policy?

Couples should be honest before making a lifelong commitment to marriage, disclosing information that could influence that decision. This includes medical and financial status, past marriages and children if any, spiritual journey and current walk in the faith, criminal history, and other "risk" factors.

In considering how honest to be in a marriage, though, it's important to examine the intent of the heart.

"Honesty" sounds pious, but can be a selfish excuse for meeting your own needs. In Suzie's case, one of her motives for demanding that Joe be "totally honest" was trying to relieve some insecurities. She was thinking, *How do I compare with my husband's past lovers? If I don't measure up, he'll be tempted again by another woman.* Her demand for even more intimate, detailed information became increasingly intense, resulting in a destructive process that had little to do with true honesty.

In the name of honesty, some people give their spouses too much information about past and present sinful actions and thoughts. To feel better about themselves, they dump their guilt feelings on their mates—unnecessarily hurting them.

Others have more sinister motives. Often the "honest" information being offered is carefully selected and intended to create anxiety in the spouse. For example, an insecure husband may try to create jealousy in his wife by describing how his female coworkers flirt with him.

Silence—choosing not to disclose all events of the day or all thoughts that cross your mind—isn't necessarily dishonest. In fact, sometimes the loving thing to do is to keep your mouth shut.

Giving a diplomatic answer in love rather than a cold, blunt "truth" is not the same as lying. In many instances, it's not particularly virtuous to "honestly" tell your husband that he's boring or not much of a lover.

And if you *do* ask, "Does this dress make me look fat?" the biblical admonition about "speaking the truth in love" (Ephesians 4:15) comes to mind. The flat truth is that the dress doesn't *make* you look fat. A more diplomatic and loving response than a simple "yes" is much advised. For example, your husband could tell you that although he thinks your blue dress looks better on you, you're very attractive no matter what dress you're wearing. "No, that dress doesn't make you look fat," he might say. "You look beautiful."

Being truthful in marriage is vital. But before demanding or disclosing "all," first be honest with yourself about your motives. Is this for the benefit of your partner and the relationship? Or is it really an attempt to immaturely or selfishly meet some of your own needs? Can those needs be met in a more emotionally healthy and spiritually mature way?

If you can't answer those questions, you may need help seeing the issues more clearly. In that case, consider seeking the insight of a wise spiritual leader or professional Christian counselor.

—*Phillip J. Swihart*

TAKING IT PERSONALLY

1. When you hear that it may not be necessary to tell your spouse everything, do you breathe a sigh of relief? Why or why not?

2. Do you have more trouble with telling the truth, or with telling it in a loving way? If the former, start by telling your mate one "inconvenient truth" about yourself this week. If the latter, write down how you'll tell your mate one "uncomfortable truth" this week in words that don't accuse, mock, or devalue him.

How Can I Get Used to Being Two Instead of One?

12

The sudden change that comes after the honeymoon can be one of life's most sobering moments. Some young couples describe this as "being hit in the face with a cold glass of water" or "being struck by lightning."

Others express it this way:

"I feel like I'm on another planet, and I want to go home!"

"I miss being able to do what I want to do, when I want to do it."

And here's a favorite that marriage therapists hear often: "If two becoming one means that I disappear as a person, forget it!"

If you feel like this, don't think you're alone or that your situation is hopeless. The following quotations illustrate the fact that the adjustment period from aloneness to togetherness is often complex:

> I figure that the degree of difficulty in combining two lives ranks somewhere between rerouting a hurricane and finding a parking place in downtown Manhattan.
>
> —*Claire Cloninger*

> I love being married. It's so great to find that one special person you want to annoy for the rest of your life.
>
> —*Rita Rudner*

Many couples wonder how the blending of two personalities and sets of ambitions, desires, and dreams could ever be expected by a wise and all-knowing God! Trying to adjust from "freedom" to partnership can be difficult and exasperating—but it's a process, not just a destination.

Here are two principles to remember when moving from independence to interdependence in marriage.

1. *The feelings are normal.* When we shift from being single to being married, we experience loss. Losing something leaves us feeling sad. But as we grow in our relationship with the person we committed to, the grief can turn to joy and contentment.

It's common for young couples to experience various levels of "buyer's remorse." That was the case with Nicole and Ted.

Nicole had waited for many years to find the right man to spend the rest of her life with. At age 33, she met Ted. Within 13 months they were married in her hometown of Atlanta.

Though she was certain Ted was the man God had chosen for her, Nicole missed her independence. Often she felt sad, conflicted, confused—wondering whether she'd made the wrong decision about marriage. She loved Ted and was thankful for him, realizing she couldn't have asked for a better man. But she struggled with having to give up her "alone time" and sense of freedom.

After praying, studying the Bible, and getting direction from Christian friends, Nicole began to see that her feelings were normal and that most people experience them. She accepted the responsibility of honoring the relationship God had given her with Ted. Each day she made conscious efforts to enjoy her relationship with her new husband in the fullest sense.

Though she occasionally needed time alone, Nicole learned to think in terms of two instead of one. When tempted to do her own thing at Ted's expense, she resisted. When it would have been easy to plop down on the couch after a hard day's work, she spent time with her husband first. Ted responded in a similar way, and their marriage developed into a bond filled with joy and intimacy.

That's how closeness and biblical oneness develop in marriages in spite of selfish tendencies. Though challenging and often confusing, the transition from independence to interdependence is absolutely vital to your union.

2. *It takes work to grow in oneness.* On a torn envelope, Sarah finds the following note left on the kitchen table one morning: "Sarah, I know you said you would like to spend time with me. I agree that we've really grown apart lately. I think we need to spend more time together, and I know you were looking forward to relaxing for a couple of evenings. Well, you get your wish. The boss called and said I have to work tonight.

"By the way, would you mind ironing my golf shorts when you get home? I have a tournament tomorrow. Oh, before I forget, tomorrow night the guys are coming over to watch the game. You don't mind, do you? And something else—I'm leaving on business to San Diego Monday. I'll be gone the rest of the week."

If Sarah is like most wives, she's thinking, *How in the world does this goofball think we're going to get close if he's always gone or having someone over?*

She's right; healthy relationships don't just evolve, they're nurtured.

Suppose Jesus had taken the attitude that closeness would "just happen" with his disciples. "Okay," He might say. "I have called you guys to be apostles. You have left everything to follow Me. But I have a lot of stress on Me; I have to save the world! So My 'alone time' is very important. Your job is to take the Gospel to the whole world, but I really think you can handle this without Me. I'll spend Saturdays with you, but the rest of the time you're on your own."

Is that how Jesus became "one" with His disciples? No. He understood the value of spending time with them, talking, teaching, dining, and experiencing happy and challenging moments together. There were times when Jesus needed to be alone, but He understood the value of being with His followers, too. In the end, He gave His life for them and they gave theirs for Him—the ultimate testimony of oneness.

If you find yourself struggling with the challenges of togetherness, here are some simple suggestions.

1. *Remember who brought you together.* God has united the two of you for a reason. It's no accident. He calls you to become one (Genesis 2:24), to honor one another (Ephesians 5:22-33), to love one another (I Corinthians 13), and to remain together until death separates you (Matthew 19:9).

2. *Change the way you think.* You're still an individual. But God has called you to leave your father and mother and unite with your spouse. That means making changes in your thinking (you belong to someone else now) as well as your behavior (you don't act like a single person anymore). Changing the way you think can change the way you feel. Start thinking like a married person, and you'll probably begin to feel like one.

3. *Educate yourself about God's desire for unity in your marriage.* Read Bible passages that emphasize the importance of oneness and unity (John 17; 1 Corinthians 7). Personalize them by inserting your

name and the name of your spouse. Pray that God will show you any attitudes and actions that stand in the way of oneness. Stop focusing on your mate's mistakes, and start working on unity by changing yourself.

4. *Learn from others.* Ask couples you know who have strong marriages how they moved from independence to interdependence. What mind-sets and habits did they adopt that worked for them?

If you asked that of Bill and Ruth, here's what they might tell you.

Bill was independent. So was Ruth. For the first three years of their marriage things were so rocky that both felt they'd made a mistake in getting married. They developed separate interests and friendships, spent little time with each other, grew apart, and even considered divorce. But because of their church background, they felt they had to stay together.

Things changed on their third anniversary. They made a commitment to each other: No matter what, they would learn how to connect and develop intimacy. They began studying the Bible and praying together, and attended every marriage conference they could find. They made spending time together a hobby; where you saw one, you'd see the other. They took up golf and skiing. For the next 20 years they would have at least one date a week.

Recently Bill and Ruth went to another marriage retreat—where they were voted Most Dedicated Couple. Their switch from aloneness to togetherness hadn't just happened. They'd intentionally drawn closer and stuck with that commitment.

They'd probably tell you that intentional intimacy is an investment that always pays off—and they'd be right.

—*Mitch Temple*

TAKING IT PERSONALLY

1. What are three things you're giving up by being married? What are three you're gaining? On balance, do you feel you're coming out ahead or behind?

2. One night this week, share a dessert with your spouse at home or in a restaurant. As you do, talk about your definitions of the following words: *independence, interdependence, aloneness,* and *togetherness.* What does sharing have to do with each of these concepts? Other than desserts, what can you share that will bring the two of you closer without "canceling out" your individuality?

SHOULD I TELL MY HUSBAND ABOUT MY PAST?

13

If you've lived in a hot, humid climate, you probably know about cockroaches. They come out at night—and can be seen to scurry when a light is suddenly turned on.

The devil is a lot like a cockroach. He does his best work in dark places, thriving on secrets. Often when the light is turned on and the truth is revealed, he loses his power and runs.

Maybe you're harboring some secrets about your past. Does that mean you should shine the spotlight on them for your spouse? Will that make your marriage better—or worse?

There are good arguments to be made for turning on the light.

First, God's design for marriage is that couples become one spiritually, physically, and emotionally. There's a greater chance for this oneness when spouses are free from the guilt and shame that often goes with past moral failures—especially hidden ones.

Second, when two people come into a marriage with unresolved hurts or failures, it affects them as individuals. When those things are intentionally hidden, it can damage the relationship in a number of ways.

For example, let's say a wife hasn't told her husband that she was sexually abused as a child. Because of that past, she finds herself unable to be playful and relaxed in the bedroom. He begins to wonder, *Is it me?*

He starts to feel insecure about his ability to fulfill his wife sexually. *Is she comparing me to someone else?* he asks himself. He remembers her dropping a hint once that she had "a past," but refusing to share the details. His self-doubt grows.

Or the husband may have had a sexual relationship in the past. He may recall it as being more fulfilling or more exciting than what he has now with his wife. He finds himself longing for those days and that person. He begins to flirt with and fantasize about someone at work, trying to recapture the past. Not wanting his wife to know about the old affair, he refuses to talk about his feelings—and the marriage continues to erode.

In cases like these, revealing secrets from the past—especially with the help of a counselor—might be constructive.

Sometimes keeping secrets seems the safest course in the beginning, but the damage emerges later. A wife who was abused as a child might not recognize her inhibitions until after she is married and intimate. By then she fears that telling her husband will hurt their sex life further. But keeping the secret makes their relationship progressively worse.

Christian counselors differ on exactly how much of the past should be revealed to a spouse. Most would agree on the following principles, however:

1. *Honesty in a relationship is an important factor in building trust.*

2. *Detail and timing are important considerations.* For instance, a wife may benefit by knowing that her husband had sex before marriage. But knowing who, what, and where might make the information too visual and hurtful and feed the imagination in a negative

way. As for timing, secrets tend to gain momentum and strength the longer you wait to reveal them. And the sting will be far less if the method and moment of telling are carefully and considerately planned rather than impulsive or offhanded.

3. *Some things are a must to share.* Examples:

- Having had a sexual partner, no matter how ashamed you may be about it, is something that should not be hidden from a mate. It should be disclosed before marriage, especially when there is a possibility of passing on a sexually transmitted disease.

- Experiencing an abortion, sexual abuse, having a baby out of wedlock, or giving up a child for adoption can cause problems in the relationship later if they haven't already—and should be discussed.

- Legal or financial "ghosts," such as lawsuits, bankruptcies, previous marriages, and criminal charges or convictions should be revealed.

4. *When in doubt about whether to share a particular secret, get help.* It's wise to seek counsel about the potential impact of turning on that spotlight. Revealing secrets of the past can strengthen a marriage—or cause insecurity and suspicion.

5. *Search your heart and know your motive.* Do you want to reveal a secret in order to hurt your spouse? To relieve yourself of guilt or shame? To just make yourself feel better? These aren't worthy motives, especially if the cost to your mate is pain and a breach in trust.

6. *Remember that you can always confess to God—and receive forgiveness.* "If we confess our sins, he is faithful and just and will forgive us our sins and purify us from all unrighteousness" (1 John 1:9).

Still not sure what to do? Here are four questions to ask yourself before sharing your past:

- Will this make my spouse feel more secure?
- Will this let my spouse know me better?
- Will this bring us closer?
- Will this prevent problems from coming up in the future?

If you're keeping a secret, be aware that it may indicate a larger problem. You may need help to deal with shame or a lack of freedom or a need for emotional healing. You may not sense enough trust in your relationship to ensure safety from judgment or rejection.

In that case, it may be time to explore those issues with a professional counselor who can give direction. It may be better to do this *before* marriage—but if you're already wed, it's not too late to do it now.

—*Romie Hurley*

TAKING IT PERSONALLY

1. What's one thing about your past that's been fun to tell your husband or fiancé about? What's one thing you've avoided bringing up? Why?

2. If you're keeping a secret about your past, what do you think would happen if you revealed it? If you can't decide whether it would be wise to share that secret, consider asking a pastor, counselor, or other trusted mentor to help you evaluate the possible impact on your marriage.

How Can I Adjust to My Husband's Personality?

14

"When she's stressed out, she talks all the time. If I get tired of talking to her after an hour or so, she gets a second wind and calls a friend!"

"He's so sensitive. I can't correct him without it making him angry. No matter what I say, he takes it wrong."

"After we leave a social event, I get so angry I can't see straight. She embarrasses me—not once, but throughout the evening."

If these statements hit home, you're not alone. Most of us have said—or at least thought—similar things about our spouses.

Couples often tell therapists that one of their toughest challenges is adjusting to a spouse's personality. Many of those people are ready to give up and resign themselves to a miserable state of existence. Others fear their situations will worsen to a point where the spouse's personality turns repulsive—and divorce will be inevitable.

So what do you do? Stay miserable? Get angry and resentful? Leave?

We suggest none of the above.

Instead, consider these facts about differences in personalities.

1. *God created us to be different.* He knew there would be a place in His plan for introverts and extroverts, for thinkers and feelers, for those who are planners and those who are spontaneous. He created

some people to be dreamers and some to be content with things as they are. "Different" doesn't automatically equal "wrong."

Proverbs 22:6 can be translated to recommend training a child "according to his bent." In other words, it's good to discover a child's distinctive personality and bring her up in a way that complements her personality instead of tearing it down. Why not apply this idea to marriages, too? Are you willing to allow your spouse the same freedom to be unique—and not the same as you?

When we realize that God planned for people to different, it's often easier to accept and adjust to a spouse's personality. It may even become possible to celebrate those differences. Otherwise, why would God create us in such variety—only to tell us to pair up and remain together for life? He's a God of compassion, not cruelty!

2. *It's easier to spot a flaw than to see a strength.* Jesus put it in terms of spying a speck in another's eye, versus seeing a log in our own (Matthew 7:3-5).

When you were dating, you probably found it easy to focus on the admirable traits of your future mate. You seemed to like the same things, enjoyed the same conversational topics, and tended to overlook each other's quirks.

Bennett, for instance, married Deb because she was such a "great communicator." Now he's annoyed because she's such a "great agitator." Dana married Marcus because he was such a "confident, strong manager." Now he's an "overconfident jerk." Juan married Paula because she was "so sweet and kind." Now he doesn't respect her because "she lets people run over her."

What changed? Why do the same personality traits we once celebrated suddenly become "logs" in our mate's eye?

During the dating process, the goal is often to conceal the "real" you and present your best side. After the wedding, the masks are dropped and unsightly reality rises to the surface. Stress, crises, pain, and disappointment also have a way of exposing what we formerly attempted to hide.

That's why it's a good idea for dating couples to go through the seasons of a year together. This allows you to see one another's imperfections. It's a test of whether you're committed enough to stay together for the rest of your lives.

"But it's too late for that," you may be saying. "We're already married!"

Then it's time to recognize the next fact.

3. *Your ability to tolerate your mate's personality changes with time.* Most of us can stand negative behavior for a while. But everyone has a limit!

Belinda, for example, could put up with Jeff's ability to make a joke out of everything—for about a year. After she became the brunt of his jokes, her level of tolerance changed. She reached a point where she despised his voice, especially his laughter.

Is that the case with you? Maybe it's not that your spouse's personality has become more of a problem; it may be that your ability to value or overlook some attributes has diminished.

Reaching your limit is no excuse for giving up on a marriage, though. Sometimes it's enough to realize that the change is in your "irritation threshold" and adjust that gauge accordingly. At other times, you may need help from a counselor to express your frustration and find a healthy tolerance level.

4. *Sometimes it's not really about personality.* Could it be that your mate has done something that deeply hurt you—and his personality has become the contention point?

That was the case with Barry. He'd always liked the fact that his wife, Wendy, was sociable and outgoing. But then he discovered that she'd been flirting with a coworker. Now Barry viewed her personality as a threat.

When your spouse hurts you, it tends to change the way you think and feel toward him. You suddenly see that person through tinted lenses, not clear ones.

If this is the case with you, healing has to occur before everyday personality issues can be objectively dealt with. Identify the real issue. Work on it—with the help of a counselor if needed. Commit to overcoming your tendency to focus on the negative aspects of your spouse's personality.

1 Corinthians 12–14 urges us to appreciate individual differences. The apostle Paul explains that every member of the "body" is valuable. Just because a part is different doesn't give us the right to despise it and set it apart from the others.

The same is true with your mate's personality. It may be different and sometimes difficult to manage. But God doesn't want this to allow division in your marriage.

One of Paul's points to the Corinthians might be summarized this way: "Learn to accept and adjust to each other, no matter what people look like or act like." That applies to husbands and wives, too.

—*Mitch Temple*

TAKING IT PERSONALLY

1. How would you describe your groom's personality? Would you have described it that way when you first met him? If your description seems to be changing, what do you think the reason is?

2. Make a list of your partner's bothersome personality traits. Then, after each trait, write a word or phrase that describes that tendency in positive terms. For example, a "pushy" husband might also be seen as "assertive" or "having leadership qualities." An "indecisive" spouse also could be "careful" or "deliberative." How could these positive qualities, like a superhero's powers, be used "for good instead of evil" in your marriage?

What Can I Do about His Irritating Habits?

15

When you got engaged, you probably thought you were marrying the person of your dreams. After the wedding day, though, you realized your spouse had some annoying habits.

Suddenly the person who could do no wrong was in need of a makeover.

Maybe you started a reforming program, only to discover that you don't have enough resources or power to change your spouse. Now your refrain sounds something like this:

"Jeremy always leaves the toilet seat up, and it annoys me in the middle of the night when I fall in. I have begged him to be more thoughtful of me."

"Bob thinks it's funny to start burping contests at the table with our boys. It is *very* embarrassing."

Chances are that you married your spouse not just because you had similarities, but also for the differences. You may have been attracted to these differences because of your need to feel completed by another person. These traits may be endearing before marriage, but can disrupt the relationship afterward.

Do you have to live with these habits? Should loving this person be enough to enable you to overlook them? And if you can't, should you feel guilty?

Being annoyed by your spouse's habits is normal. The key is to learn to work together to change the habits that can be changed and learn to accept those that can't.

First, ask yourself why you want your spouse to change. Is it for your own good only? Might the change make you feel better, but cause your mate to feel imprisoned? Or is the change to help eliminate behaviors that keep your spouse from growing emotionally and spiritually? In other words, are you helping to set your partner free or just restricting his freedom?

If changing the habit would truly benefit both of you, change may be worth trying. But keep these guidelines in mind:

1. *Address the problem honestly.* "Honey, it bothers me when you burp at the table. It teaches the children a bad habit, and it's rude and offensive to guests."

2. *Explain the benefit of change.* "Eating at the table will be more pleasant for all of us. The boys will also respect your table manners and you'll be a good testimony to our guests."

3. *Don't command change.* "You're such a slob at the table. Stop being so messy." Instead, *request* change. Your spouse will respond more favorably.

4. *Don't attack your mate.* "You are a horrible listener. It's no wonder no one talks to you." When you attack your spouse, you crush his spirit—and don't get much cooperation. Confront the problem; don't attack the person.

5. *Discuss ways to bring about change.* Change is hard. Let your spouse know that you're on his side. Help him find ways to change those habit patterns. If the problem is overeating, for instance, go

with your spouse to the gym, cook healthy meals, and go out to eat less often. Be your mate's advocate.

6. *Encourage your spouse's growth.* "You're doing a great job. I'm really proud of the effort I see. Thank you for your dedication to making this change."

7. *Recognize that change takes time.* Be patient with your spouse. Praise little steps that you see. Everyone wants to feel successful. So don't discourage your mate with comments like, "This is taking forever. How many more times do we have to deal with this?" Discouragement stunts growth, but encouragement goes a long way in motivating change. Let your spouse know you're in this together for the long haul.

8. *Focus on your spouse's good habits, not just the irritating ones.* "John makes me mad," one wife said. "I have asked him to clean the tub after each use. He never does.

"Last week when I was getting ready for work, I received a call from the hospital. John was in an accident. As I quickly dressed to go to the hospital, I noticed the dirt ring in the bathtub. I began to sob. The Lord brought to mind all the wonderful qualities of my husband, and I felt so petty for complaining about the ring in the tub. When John came home several days later, I found myself sitting in the bathroom and thanking the Lord that I would have more time with John and more rings in the tub. I was reminded of Philippians 4:8: 'Whatever is honorable, pure, just, lovely . . . think on these things.'

"When I see the ring now, I turn my thoughts to the wonderful qualities of my husband and the annoyance of that ring in the tub disappears."

9. *Pray for your spouse.* God is ultimately the one who makes change possible in any of us. So pray for your mate's efforts. And

since some behaviors may never change, ask God to give you grace to accept the differences between you and your spouse.

10. *Seek to change the habit, not the person.* It's possible to help your spouse drop an irritating habit—as long as it's the habit you're trying to change. If you're trying to alter your spouse's personality or temperament, you'll be fighting a losing battle that will end in frustration for both of you.

Take Susan and Lee, for example. Susan, an extremely social person, loves to stay after church to talk, is the last to leave a party, and likes to be the center of attention. In contrast, her husband, Lee, is reserved, prefers to be in the background, and is exhausted by socializing. Lee has learned to go to parties with Susan out of love for her. But she can't expect him to become a fan of social gatherings. She needs to appreciate his willingness to go with her and not try to make him the extrovert she is.

If you follow the aforementioned guidelines and don't meet with success, it's time to ask yourself whether the battle is worth it. Some habits are so engrained that if they don't involve moral issues or character flaws, it may be best to live with them. Bringing them up repeatedly may lead only to more bitterness and conflict.

Keep praying for your spouse. And when you think of him, focus on his positive traits—instead of that irritating habit.

—*Sheryl DeWitt*

Taking It Personally

1. How much do you think you'd have to pay your groom to give up his most irritating habit? How much would he have to pay you to ignore it?

2. If you've tried to discuss this issue before, what hap-pened? Pick one of the ten pre-ceding guidelines that could make a positive difference when you bring the issue up this week.

Why Isn't Marriage the Way
I Thought It Would Be?

16

On their honeymoon, Ed and Renee spent hours gazing into each other's eyes— contemplating how they'd spend their next 50 years. They decided to write those plans down as a road map for the future.

But before long, those plans hit several speed bumps.

Ed lost his job.

Renee was diagnosed with diabetes.

Habits that seemed cute at first became annoying.

When they had a son, Renee decided to stay home—which tightened the family purse strings. Ed worked more to compensate, further reducing their time together. When she voiced concern, it only seemed to irritate him.

They still loved each other. But this wasn't how either of them had written the script on their honeymoon.

You might find yourself wondering if *your* early dreams of marital bliss were more illusion than reality. Why isn't marriage turning out the way you planned?

In premarital counseling, couples often explore their expectations of marriage. But what does that mean? Are expectations the way you think your marriage *will* look, or the way you *want* it to look? The two can be very different!

People draw their marital expectations from two wells. One is courtship. If dating was wonderful and starry-eyed, why would you expect marriage to be otherwise? *If spending 20 hours a week brings us such joy,* you might think, *more time together as husband and wife could only be better!*

But think back to your courtship. Wasn't it largely a mirage?

What did you do when you didn't want to be alone? You got dressed up and did fun things together. What did you do when you were tired of talking? You went home. How did you deal with financial decisions? You made them on your own.

When you were dating, there were some built-in escape valves in your relationship. Now that you're married, there's no other home to go to. Your spouse's finances are yours, and vice versa.

By its nature, courtship allows a couple to live in denial. Marriage makes that posture much more difficult to maintain.

The other well of marital expectations is the marriage you saw firsthand when you were growing up.

That relationship provided one of two images for you to view. Either the marriage didn't seem worth duplicating, or it did.

Even if the marriage you saw was conflicted and unhappy, you may have believed things would be different for you. Without that hope, the decision to remain single would have seemed pretty appealing. But simply raising your expectations won't make your marriage better than that of your parents. You need to face past hurts and disappointments, perhaps with the help of a counselor or pastor. That may not have the same thrill that romance does, but it makes it more likely that you'll experience a fulfilling and romantic marriage.

On the other hand, you may have been fortunate enough to see a model of marriage worth replicating. For that you can rejoice! But there's a pitfall there, too. You may be locked into thinking that the way you saw Mom and Dad relate is the only healthy way for a marriage to function.

For example, let's say that your parents were both even-tempered; decisions came easily for them. You or your spouse might be more opinionated and need to discuss matters longer. That's okay, even though it's different. There are many styles in marriage that can be healthy.

Parents can affect your marital expectations in other ways, too. That was true with Tom and Jill.

Tom's expectations about marriage weren't being met. Through reading and counseling he finally recognized that those expectations were an effort to cope with a painful childhood. Growing up, he'd often been under his mother's controlling thumb. He'd brought into marriage a vow that he'd never get close enough to his wife to let her control him as Mom had. As a result, he'd never gotten close enough to truly connect with Jill.

Tom had to work through his hurts before he could begin to relate to Jill in a more meaningful way. The two of them met period-ically over coffee with a seasoned couple in their church, learning what they might expect in each new stage of marriage.

They still have struggles. But Tom is learning more about God's expectations for their marriage. Unless he depends on God for the ability to love Jill, he doesn't have a prayer to make it happen. He's also learning that by staying true to his marriage, he's growing in ways he never thought possible.

Tom brought his own expectations to marriage, but God had a better idea.

If your expectations about marriage have been unrealistic, it's time to challenge them. But if you do, and still have concerns, consider the possibility that the problem might not be your expectations. You might have a problem in your marriage.

Harboring unrealistic expectations doesn't mean that everything else in a marriage is on track. Your qualms might be slightly off target, but they could be early warning signs about issues that will cause more trouble if you don't resolve them. Talk about them with your spouse in a respectful way; see whether the two of you can address them. If that fails, look to a pastor or counselor for help.

—*Glenn Lutjens*

TAKING IT PERSONALLY

1. Would you say "the honeymoon is over" in your relationship? Why or why not?

2. Think of an older couple who could help you form realistic expectations about what might happen during the next few years of your marriage. Ask them whether they'd be willing to meet with you once or twice to describe the stages they've gone through. Then talk with your spouse about three things you can do to prepare for the likely challenges ahead.

How Should We Divide Up the Chores?

17

When you fell in love, was the question of how to divide up the chores on your radar screen? Probably not.

But now that you're married, chores are one thing you can't escape. The daily routine for all but the very wealthy consists of activities like cooking meals, doing the dishes, washing clothes, maintaining household appliances, repairing the car(s), handling the finances, parenting the kids (if any), feeding the animals (if any), choosing insurance, and cleaning the house or apartment. Some chores pop up right after the honeymoon; others emerge over time.

It's common to think in terms of "male" and "female" chores. But should a wife automatically be in charge of shower curtains, while her husband specializes in replacing shower heads?

Christian couples may tend to think such male/female distinctions are biblical rather than traditional. But the Bible doesn't specifically support the notion that, for example, only women must cook and only men must calculate the budget and finances. After all, Jacob prepared the stew that Esau ate (Genesis 25); the "wife of noble character" in Proverbs 31 dealt with business concerns.

How you feel about dividing up chores has a lot to do with the way your parents handled this question.

Steve assumes the husband is supposed to handle all the chores outside the home and the wife handles those inside. That's the way his parents did things.

His wife Abby, on the other hand, had a father who master-minded the family finances, vacuumed the floors, and did the gardening. She expects Steve to do the same.

Down the street, Greg recalls how his mother balanced the checkbook and painted the walls. He thinks his wife Tyra should follow that pattern.

Tyra, meanwhile, had a father who loved to cook. Why, she wonders, won't Greg follow in his footsteps?

Differences like these lead one spouse to feel the other isn't "pulling his or her weight" when it comes to household duties.

One young husband and wife, married only six months, came to a counselor because they'd been arguing constantly over chores. The husband was upset because his wife "wasted time" and didn't get as much done as he expected. The wife was resentful because her husband didn't feel he should have to help at home after putting in a hard day at the office.

That couple wasn't unusual. Anger and arguments over sharing responsibilities often bring spouses into counseling for resolution.

So is there a right answer to the question of dividing up chores?

A quick response might be to suggest adopting the Fox News motto, "Fair and Balanced." But what does that mean?

Here are more specific guidelines that may help prevent or bridge areas of conflict when it comes to chores.

1. *Think positively.* Most husbands and wives enter marriage expecting to share the load to some degree. Figuring out how to make the

sharing balanced and appropriate is not only desirable, but possible.

2. *Consider the rewards.* When husband and wife work outside the home, tackling chores together lifts the load. It gives you more time for individual activities. It gives you more time together.

3. *Concentrate on giftedness, not gender.* Rather than emphasizing "male" and "female" chores, talk about which jobs you enjoy or don't mind doing. Which do you have a knack for? Which would you prefer not to do?

4. *Allow for exceptions.* Helping each other out with chores during times of stress, busyness, or illness is very much appreciated by a spouse. It also tends to be reciprocated.

5. *Write it down.* Making a list of what needs to be done is essential. It's too easy to forget who's supposed to do what.

6. *Stay flexible.* No matter how fair and equal things seem at the start, you may have to make adjustments along the way. One spouse who was at home may begin a full-time job. Another may endure serious illness or injury.

7. *Don't go strictly by the numbers.* Fair and equal doesn't necessarily mean "one for you, one for me." Remember that some chores are more difficult and time-consuming than others.

8. *Chart yours, mine, and ours.* A busy, young husband and wife struggled to balance their desire for fun with the reality of day-to-day duties. They developed a simple chart that made the "to do" list look less intimidating—and more equally distributed.

MATT'S CHORES
1. Painting the house
2. Repairs on vehicles
3. Developing a budget

OUR CHORES

1. Care for the garden
2. Cleaning the house
3. Planning vacations

MARY'S CHORES

1. Buying groceries, fixing meals
2. Balancing checkbook
3. Home decorating

Dividing up chores is an opportunity for cooperation rather than conflict. A key to the challenge of marriage is striving to understand each other and seeking to meet each other's needs—and this is a great area in which to practice.

Even the act of discussing and dividing up what needs to be accomplished can lessen conflict. If you find yourself stuck in these issues, though, don't hesitate to seek assistance from a more experienced couple or a counselor.

—*Wilford Wooten*

TAKING IT PERSONALLY

1. Share with your husband (or husband-to-be) how your parents
   divided up the following chores: taking out the garbage, cleaning
   the bathroom, vacuuming
   floors, shopping for groceries, cooking, filling out
   tax returns, unplugging the
   sink, washing clothes, changing
   diapers, balancing the checkbook,
   and attending parent-teacher confer-
   ences. What patterns were the same on both
   sides of the family? Which were different?

2. Make a chart like the one Matt and Mary made. Then take it
   a step further, discussing how often each duty needs to be
   performed—and under what circumstances one spouse will step
   in and do the other's tasks.

What If My Spouse Won't Take the "Right" Role?

18

Many husbands and wives would like to "recast" their spouses in the "right" roles, as if their marriages were stage plays. These adjustments, they think, are the gateway to happiness.

"If only he would be the spiritual leader, things would be better in the house."

"If only she would cook and clean, there would be less stress around here."

The reality is that no one can force another to take on the "right" role. But the good news is that many spouses, if given the opportunity, will shoulder the necessary roles to make a marriage successful.

Two people who are truly committed to one another will do what's necessary to "fill in the gaps" in their relationship. If one is forced or nagged into assuming a needed role, though, the tendency for him or her is to lose interest in taking on the "right" part.

When Barb married Philip, she assumed that he was handy. She expected him to fix whatever needed fixing around the house or on the cars. Little did she know that Philip wasn't skilled in these areas. He'd never been shown how to do simple home or auto repairs.

She began to criticize him, which made him even more disinterested in helping. In fact, it began to disconnect him from her altogether.

Philip needed to be encouraged by his wife. He needed the time and opportunity to learn what he hadn't been taught. Instead, he felt ridiculed and hurt.

You and your spouse can avoid that pitfall by listening to each other's views on what "right" and "wrong" roles are. You'll need to do it patiently and respectfully.

Which of you should keep track of relatives' birthdays? Who should research where to send charitable donations? Which of you should take kids to the doctor, hang pictures on the walls, or ask the neighbor to turn down his music?

Only the two of you can answer those questions. But the following principles can help guide your discussion of which roles are right for you.

1. *The right role brings you together instead of driving you apart.* Remember that you're dividing responsibilities, not your relationship. It's usually not helpful to assign roles "because you're the man" or "because that's women's work," for instance. If your "one flesh" (Genesis 2:24) team is to work, you need to work together.

2. *The right role takes your strengths and weaknesses into account.* Look at each other's assets and liabilities; try to base roles on the use of strengths. For example, if one of you is more interested and more effective in maintaining a checkbook, that person should assume the responsibility.

3. *The right role allows for flexibility.* The flexibility starts during the discussion process. Try to negotiate without "hardheadedness."

Think of this as an exercise in togetherness, a way to cooperate in accomplishing vital tasks. Flexibility should continue as you carry out your responsibilities; for instance, if one spouse has handled all cooking and cleaning but takes a job outside the home, it's unrealistic to expect him or her to keep up with all the old duties as well as the new ones.

4. *The right role may be sacrificial.* There are some jobs nobody wants—but they need to be done anyway. Few of us aspire to clean the toilets, keep raccoons out of the garbage cans, or take the baby's temperature in the middle of the night. Review each other's strengths to determine which spouse comes closer to being the "expert" in an area, but don't expect an exact match. This will take humility and cooperation from both parties; if only one person (or neither) is willing to sacrifice, resentment and division will most likely make their way into the relationship. If this is the case for you, enlist a pastor or counselor to help break the stalemate.

When it comes to getting your spouse to take on a needed role, encouragement can go a long way. Cheer with your words as well as with hugs and smiles. Noticing your mate's efforts creates an atmosphere of support and teamwork.

Husbands especially need to feel appreciated, and thrive when complimented on their efforts to take on the "right" role. Wives also enjoy compliments, of course, but tend to get the most satisfaction from seeing their husbands help around the house without expecting anything in return and on their own initiative.

It's common in Christian counseling for a wife to ask, "What should I do when my husband won't assume the role of spiritual leader?" Christian husbands who avoid that role may do so because they feel anxious, self-conscious, unworthy, or overwhelmed by the prospect.

The counselor may respond with questions like these:

"How are you being a part of the solution?"

"Are you encouraging your husband, or are you nagging and putting him down because he won't assume the role?"

"When he reads Scripture, do you frequently correct him while he's trying?"

"What will happen if your husband never assumes the role?"

The answers to these questions are very important. They help the wife to focus on what can be controlled and changed.

Look for each other's spiritual strengths. Build a healthy spiritual life together. If your spouse isn't interested in that, you may need to assume a leadership role. Seek guidance from your pastor as you do so. Look for a mentor whose spiritual life you admire. Make it a point to renew yourself spiritually on a daily basis, and to find new and exciting ways to bring the Bible to life for your children if you have any. Keep praying for your spouse's spiritual growth, too.

You can't *make* your spouse take on the "right" role. But you can work on the kind of relationship that makes it easier to assume the roles that are best for both of you.

That was the case with Greg and Laura, who'd just married. Both had managed their money wisely as singles; Greg liked learning about the subject, and Laura had a bachelor's degree in mathematics. She also seemed more organized about maintaining her checkbook and paid close attention to deadlines.

At first Greg wanted to be the family financial expert. Soon, though, he realized Laura was the best one for the job.

Laura, meanwhile, realized that she didn't know—or care to know—much about investing. So Greg assumed that responsibility.

This arrangement worked because Greg and Laura admitted their weaknesses and acknowledged their spouse's strengths. Their relationship allowed them to work together in the "right" roles.

Finding the "right" roles in a marriage takes honest self-assessment, time, experimentation, and a willingness to adjust. It also takes a dedication to each other that's bigger than the logistics of who does what.

—*Daniel Huerta*

TAKING IT PERSONALLY

1. What issues regarding roles do you wish you'd discussed earlier in your relationship? Is there any reason you can't start talking about them now? Explain.

2. If you'd like your husband to take on a new role, are you willing to change yours accordingly? For instance, if you want him to be more of a spiritual leader in your home, will you become more of a follower? If you want him to start making the bed, will you give up the title of "bed-making expert" and let him do it his way? How will you communicate this willingness to him?

Do We Have to Have a Budget?

19

For many couples, "budget" is a scary word.

What bothers you about the idea of having a budget? Is it fear that there won't be enough money? Is it not liking to be told what to do, even by a list of numbers? Does budgeting sound too complicated?

Jennifer and Josh have been told that they ought to have a budget. They're not sure they like the idea. Here are some benefits they need to consider.

1. *A budget establishes a spending plan.* When Josh and Jennifer decide to go to a movie, it will come out of their entertainment fund—with no "guilt trip" attached. When they choose to buy a toaster, they can take money from the discretionary fund or the personal spending fund. That's because they'll have decided in advance what to do. Having a plan gives you options, and having options means freedom.

2. *A budget encourages saving.* If they follow their budget, at the end of the month Jennifer and Josh will have put $100 in savings. Without a budget, that fund may not accumulate.

3. *A budget reduces stress.* With a budget, both Jennifer and Josh will understand how much money is available each month. When

they respect the system, finance won't be a primary focus of conflict—which it often is early in marriage. As I Timothy 6:10 puts it, "For the love of money is a root of all kinds of evil." You and your spouse want to love each other, not money—and not allow money to cause division.

4. *A budget allows for the unexpected.* Emergency expenses can be overwhelming, especially in a new marriage. Setting aside funds for surprise expenditures can help reduce pressure on both Josh and Jennifer. Emergencies are traumatic enough without the chaos that can result from not having a "rainy day" account.

5. *A budget encourages giving.* Having a budget can help Josh and Jennifer to honor God with what's already His. Jesus said, "Do not store up for yourselves treasures on earth, where moth and rust destroy, and where thieves break in and steal. But store up for yourselves treasures in heaven, where moth and rust do not destroy, and where thieves do not break in and steal. For where your treasure is, there your heart will be also" (Matthew 6:19-21).

Budgeting that allows for generosity will help Josh and Jennifer discover how giving to God's work promotes peace and joy and enhances their closeness to Him.

6. *A budget discourages debt.* Having a plan and sticking to it will keep Josh and Jennifer from overcommitting themselves financially. Debt is a burden on any marriage. If you're in debt, formulating a plan to eliminate it could be a gift to your relationship. Crown Financial Ministries (www.crown.org) is one organization that provides advice on debt reduction as well as budgeting.

7. *A budget can be flexible.* Josh and Jennifer, like many couples, fear a budget will be a straitjacket. But financial freedom can be

expanded by constantly evaluating the budget. Maybe there's a better car insurance plan. Perhaps refinancing the mortgage to save interest is an option. Or Josh and Jennifer may want to take half the money from the "dining out" budget for the next year and put it into a "save up for vacation" account.

8. *A budget can encourage spouses to submit to the same authority—God.* To set up a budget, you have to set priorities. Discussing those and seeking God's direction in the process can go a long way toward financial harmony. If Josh and Jennifer look to God and His Word for guidance, they won't be competing to be in charge of each other's spending habits.

When you get right down to it, a budget is simply a financial plan. The budget Jennifer and Josh design will have a chance to work only if they respect each other and are willing to give up "entitlement issues." In other words, Josh can't insist on going on a hunting trip using part of the rent money. Jennifer can't buy on impulse and then accuse Josh of not making enough money.

Let's say Jennifer and Josh decide to try a budget based on their annual gross income of $46,000. Here's how they might divide their monthly expenses.

Mortgage or rent	$900
Utilities	$100
Transportation	$140
Insurance (home)	$100
Insurance (cars)	$200
Insurance (health)	$150
Insurance (life)	$ 50

Phone	$100
Cable	$ 30
Food	$300
Discretionary (entertainment)	$200
Personal spending	$100
Giving	$300
Savings	$100
Emergency fund (e.g., auto repair)	$300
Taxes (income)	$763
TOTAL	$3,833

Your categories and amounts may vary. But if you want the freedom of planned spending, freedom from financial chaos in emergencies, freedom from debt, and joy in giving, a budget probably is for you.

Living on a budget means learning to live on less than your income. It may involve discipline, planning, and sacrifice. But it could be one way to experience genuine freedom on the "Monday mornings" of your marriage.

—*Betty Jordan*

Taking It Personally

1. What scares, repels, or confuses you about budgeting? Which of the benefits listed is most convincing to you?

2. Using as a model the budget Josh and Jennifer made, prepare a monthly plan of your own. Decide how you'll keep track of how much you have left in each category—either by putting cash in envelopes representing the categories, or simply by maintaining a running tally on paper or computer. Plan to review the process in three months or less to see how it's working.

How Often Is Normal?

20

Shifting uncomfortably at one end of the living room couch, Brady avoided the gaze of his wife, Deanna, who sat at the other end.

"I don't think I'm . . . *abnormal* to want sex several times a week," he said, keeping his voice down. "But the way you act, you'd think I was some kind of pervert."

"No, I don't think that, Brady." Deanna couldn't keep the tears from spilling down her cheeks now. "It's just that with the baby and everything, I don't have anything left to give at the end of the day."

Brady got up and started pacing in front of the fireplace, his arms extended in exasperation. "We waited to get married—and you know how hard that was. I thought once it was 'legal' we'd want to do it all the time!"

Brady and Deanna aren't the only couple clashing over the question of how often they "should" have sex. The issue usually comes up when spouses' expectations about the frequency of intercourse don't match—a common complaint.

Researchers don't all agree on how often the average couple has sex. According to *Understanding Human Sexuality* by Janet Shibley Hyde and John D. DeLamater (McGraw-Hill, 1997), the largest percentage of married couples reporting in a study said they had intercourse three times a week. But as an article on the MayoClinic.com Web site points out, "Statistics on sexual behavior can be quite misleading. For example, a couple might read that the average married couple has intercourse three times a week. They may not be aware, however, that this average includes a wide range. The frequency of intercourse might range from zero for some to 15 or 20 times a week for others. Therefore, even if their frequency of inter-course is more or less than three times a week, their behavior is within the range of normal human experience."

Oversimplified averages can create anxious reactions. If you have sex more than twice a week, does that make you abnormal? If you have sex twice a month, is your marriage less healthy than most?

Here are five things to remember when you and your spouse aren't sure whether the frequency of your sexual activity is "normal."

1. *Every couple is different.* Frequency of sexual activity can be a measure of the general health of a marriage. But there's no numerical standard that applies to every couple.

Factors like gender, individual expectations, developmental maturity as a couple, and cultural differences all affect the numbers. In early marriage these variables are especially evident, as the honey-moon effect wanes and we find out where our own "normal" will land on the scale.

During the first years of marriage, it's especially important to dis-cern which sources of information about sexuality can be trusted. You can't gauge what's normal from the impressions given by many TV shows and movies, for instance. Sex also deserves the honor of privacy, which discourages comparing notes with friends on what works for them. In addition to seeking wise, godly counsel from a mentor, you might find helpful several books by Christians. You'll find some listed among the resources at the end of this guide.

2. *Quality precedes quantity.* The parenting myth of "quality time" over "quantity time" happily is being debunked. When it comes to sex, though, quality really is more important than quantity. This doesn't mean either spouse has an excuse to cop out of marital responsibilities in the bedroom. It's a call to excellence.

If you're dissatisfied with your sex life, instead of first complaining about the frequency, examine the quality. Ask yourself, "Would *I* want to be married to me?" Consider how well you meet your spouse's sexual needs; find out what changes might be in order. Once communication increases and needs are satisfied, increased frequency usually isn't far behind.

3. *There's a time to serve.* Sadly, a lot of factors in our broken world can leave one or both spouses needing special consideration. Sexual trauma, addiction, abortion, and disease affect our sexuality in profound ways. Recovery is often slow, requiring patience and understanding from both partners.

A woman's reproductive cycle also requires understanding from her husband. Premenstrual syndrome (PMS), menstruation, and pregnancy—not to mention breastfeeding and caring for infants and young children—can leave a wife drained physically and emotionally. At these times, a husband will do well to keep the "big picture" in mind, remembering that sexual intimacy may suffer temporarily—but his sacrificial service will yield fruit for the relationship in the future.

4. *Be intentional.* Impulsive, spontaneous sex can be great, but it tends to fall by the wayside as jobs, mortgages, and children enter the

picture. It's certainly possible (and preferable) to keep a fun-loving chemistry going throughout marriage, but depending on that alone is often not enough.

If you give your spouse only the leftovers of your time and energy, neither of you will be sexually satisfied. Planning a time and place for intimacy seems anything but intimate, but the lack of negotiation can lead to lack of fulfillment—or worse, to looking elsewhere for it.

5. *Sex is a picture.* Scripture paints a beautiful portrait of Christ's return for His beloved Bride, the church. Our spiritual union with Him is echoed in every aspect of our earthly marriages, including sexuality. For example, a healthy husband and wife will want to focus on the quality of their sexual relationship, not just how often they have sex. It's about the relationship—not the numbers.

It can be easy to forget that, as Brady did during that confrontation with Deanna. He remembered it later, when the two of them dropped the baby off at her mother's on the way to their weekly date.

At their favorite Italian restaurant they drifted into small talk, both regretting the earlier conflict.

"Hon, I'm sorry I raised my voice to you earlier," Brady finally blurted, then glanced around to make sure other diners weren't looking his way. "I think I've just been feeling like you don't want me like you used to. I mean, I know in my head there are other reasons. My heart just doesn't always pay attention."

Deanna fished in her purse for more tissues. "I do want to show you how much I love you," she whispered, hoping the people around her didn't notice her tears. "I get caught up in the diapers and the feedings and everything else. I'm glad we've at least got our date night to remind us to focus on us, too."

—*Rob Jackson*

TAKING IT PERSONALLY

1. In a perfect world, how often would you and your husband have sex? How do you think he would answer that? If these questions are tough to answer, why is that?

2. Have you and your spouse talked about the "how often" issue? If so, who brought it up and why? If not, why not? If you need a way to bring it up, try combining it light-heartedly with a couple of other, less volatile subjects—like how often to check the oil in your car and how frequently to mop the kitchen floor.

What If We Don't Like the Same Things Sexually?

21

Jill didn't know what to say when she opened Mark's gift. The pretty package had been a total surprise. "It just made me think of you," he'd told her.

Judging by the size of the box, she'd thought it might be a new scarf or a sampler of chocolates. The last thing she'd expected was this lace teddy.

Didn't Mark know she wasn't the lingerie type? She could imagine how big her thighs would look in this thing.

Sometimes she thought they'd never see eye to eye when it came to sex. They'd been married only a year, and already their differences were clear. What would things be like five years from now—if they made it that far?

Jill and Mark are learning to their chagrin that sexual arousal is a very individual matter. One spouse wants the lights on; the other wants it dark. Each partner prefers a certain touch, a certain time, even a certain temperature.

When you and your mate like "different strokes," what should you do? Here are five suggestions.

1. *Discover your comfort zone.* You probably would expect to negotiate which colors to paint the rooms of your new house, or

whether to serve tofu for dinner. Why be surprised if you encounter some differences in your sexual desires? As you discover your "comfort zone" as a couple, keep in mind that this process is a normal developmental task for every marriage.

Some argue that this process could be helped along by living together before the wedding. But statistics prove otherwise. Studies reveal that, instead of increasing sexual compatibility, premarital cohabitation actually boosts the likelihood of sexually transmitted disease, sexual dysfunction, codependency, divorce, and loss of trust. Clearly, becoming one flesh is sacred for a reason.

2. *Be a servant.* Your approach to sex should mirror your approach to marriage in general: "Serve one another in love" (Galatians 5:13).

Solomon referred to his wife as "my sister, my bride" (Song of Solomon 4:10). Can you keep the perspective of being brother and sister in Christ as well as being spouses? A servant's attitude can guard against letting differences in bed become a power struggle or cause for resentment.

Basic issues of preference, such as whether to have the lights on or which positions are more pleasurable, are good opportunities to listen and learn what pleases your spouse. If something causes one partner embarrassment or discomfort, he or she should never feel pressured to participate. It's also important that both partners express preferences without criticism and without judging each other.

3. *Discern moral issues.* Each of us enters marriage with an "arousal template" or set of stimuli that triggers sexual interest. If you've had prior sexual relationships or exposure to pornography, for example, unhealthy appetites may have been added to your template.

Even between consenting spouses, certain sexual behaviors are still wrong. For example, a husband may claim that pornography helps his sex life—but its use actually constitutes an act of adultery (Matthew 5:27-28). Any sexual practices that are demeaning or physically harmful will damage true intimacy as well as violate biblical guidelines. Work together to find *what's* right instead of fighting over *who's* right.

4. *Address trauma or addiction.* If conflict over sex escalates beyond simply choosing a "menu" you both like, it's possible there's a history of sexual trauma for one or both spouses. Associating shame or fear with sexuality is a powerful dynamic to overcome. Severe trauma can produce a condition known as Sexual Aversion Disorder. Survivors of childhood sexual abuse often need the help of a professional Christian counselor to restore a healthy sex life.

Addiction to pornography, fantasy, and masturbation can put another big roadblock in a couple's path. Seeing sex as forbidden, dirty, or provocative leads to unhealthy fixations. A spouse may feel the addict is "not really there" during sex or that he or she is being used as a sexual object rather than loved intimately. Childhood sexual trauma is a frequent precursor to pornography addiction, and professional therapy is a critical tool for recovery.

5. *Talk about sex.* No matter what your sexual differences are, the first step to connecting well sexually is to do so verbally. Sometimes discussing these issues during intimacy can evoke feelings of shame or embarrassment. So it's often a good idea to wait and discuss it later, outside the bedroom.

Once you've established a healthy pattern of communication, conversation can even contribute to the sexual experience. You and your spouse can connect physically and at deeper levels as well. Talking about your love and desire for your spouse will build a safe, satisfying experience for both partners before, during, and after sexual intercourse.

Let's get back to Jill and Mark. Jill's still standing there with the gift of lingerie. What should she do?

Mark hesitates, seeing her expression. "I—I hope I didn't shock you with the present," he stammers. "I know it's not your usual style, but I really thought you'd look beautiful in it."

Jill smooths the gold ribbon on the box. She starts thinking about how Mark has shown her in so many ways that she is God's gift to him.

A shy smile plays across her lips. She even quits worrying about how her thighs would look in this outfit.

Okay, she thinks. *As long as he treasures me like this, I'll wrap his gift any way he likes.*

—Rob Jackson

TAKING IT PERSONALLY

1. If you're not married yet, does the possibility that you'll have to work out your sexual differences after the wedding make you nervous, or sound like a good chance to get closer? Why?

2. If you're married, what differences have you noticed in the ways you and your husband approach sex? Have you talked about this? If so, what happened? If not, it may be easier to bring up the subject if the two of you first read the Song of Solomon from the Bible. See whether you can find at least half a dozen possible references to lovemaking, and talk about whether those "techniques" appeal to you.

Why Don't We Speak the Same Language?

22

Are men and women really from different planets?

Any marriage counselor can provide tons of examples of husbands and wives who, having lived together for 20 or 30 years (let alone just 4 or 5), are in some ways a complete mystery to each other. The obvious answer is that God chose to wire males and females very differently. Some would even suggest that this illustrates His sense of humor.

It's possible that the communication gender gap lies in how messages are perceived. But the style and content of the messages themselves differ, too. Men tend to use language to transmit information, report facts, fix problems, clarify status, and establish control. Women are more likely to view language as a means to greater intimacy, stronger or richer relationships, and fostering cooperation rather than competition.

In other words, it's "debate vs. relate." That means you and your spouse may be tuned in to very different "meanings" in what each of you is saying. This provides fertile ground for misunderstanding, hurt feelings, and conflict. What one of you thinks is the other's "hidden meaning" can be 180 degrees out of phase with what the speaker really intends to communicate.

This can easily lead to distorted conclusions about the other person's motivations.

She's an unreasonable, demanding nag who won't leave me alone to watch the football game, he thinks.

He's an insensitive, domineering bore who doesn't have a clue about my feelings and doesn't want one, she tells herself.

Nancy and Ralph are having this kind of conflict.

Nancy sits in the counselor's office in tears. Ralph, her husband of three years, sits stony-faced, two feet away on the same couch, his arms crossed over his chest. The atmosphere is thick with her fury and his defiance.

She begins the session with a litany of Ralph's alleged failures, the worst being his neglect of her needs. He is, she says, "never home." Self-employed, he works long hours and takes frequent business trips. Sometimes he leaves on the refrigerator lists of things for her to get done while he's gone. He also leaves her with the care of a one-year-old.

When he's home, she says, he's either restoring an antique car or wanting to jump into bed for a quick sexual romp—for which he seems to have plenty of energy. When she's dead tired and turns him down, he pouts and sometimes storms out to the garage and his beloved Chevy. She notes with undisguised sarcasm that he's always too tired to just talk to her.

The final straw: Last week, on her birthday, he was gone on another business trip. She feels abandoned and unloved.

When Ralph finally speaks up, it's to say that things are usually much more peaceful in the garage than in the bedroom. At least the Chevy doesn't treat him like he's some dirty old man.

He can't understand why Nancy is so angry about his long hours at work. She seems to him to have no concept of what it takes to earn the money needed each month to pay the bills. This is how a husband and father takes care of—loves—his family. And why would she be upset about his efforts to organize on a list the chores that need to be done when he's out of town?

When she caustically remarks that she isn't one of his employees, it makes no sense to him. What does that have to do with their family life? Of course he loves her, he says. Look at everything he does to be a good husband.

Standing outside looking in, it seems easy to see that when it comes to understanding each other's languages, Nancy and Ralph are missing each other by a mile. In many respects, they exemplify stereotypical male-female struggles with differences in communication.

Of course, one size never fits all. Females don't all fit neatly into one communication-style box and males into another. Some men can be quite nurturing and emotionally empathic in their language; some women are aggressive and task-oriented in theirs.

Still, you needn't be surprised if you and your spouse sometimes seem to need a translator. In his book *How Do You Say "I Love You"?* (InterVarsity Press, 1977), Dr. Judson Swihart notes, "Often the wife comes in [to the marriage] speaking French and the husband speaking German—in an emotional sense. Unless you hear love expressed in a language that you can understand emotionally, it will have little value." The author goes on to say, "Fi uoy era gniog ot etacinummoc na edutitta fo evol drawot ruoy esuops, you must learn to speak his or her language."

It's hard to do that if, like too many couples, you enter marriage focused on being loved rather than on giving love. Try making it your goal not to change your spouse but to adapt to his style of communication. Turn your attention to hearing the heart of your partner rather than to the frustration you may feel about not being heard or understood.

If you feel stuck, and that your marriage is in a hole that just gets deeper, do something about it. Make a date with each other once a week to try a communication exercise. For example, the wife talks for ten minutes about feelings or issues she has; the husband does nothing but listen. He may respond only with, "I don't understand; could you restate that?" or "What I hear you saying is . . ."

Then he talks for ten minutes and she listens. She can ask only for clarification or affirmation that she's hearing him accurately.

At the end of the exercise, neither of you is allowed to try to "straighten the other one out," react angrily to something you didn't want to hear, or debate the issue. During the next such "date," the husband will talk first and the wife second.

Other approaches to getting "unstuck" include attending a well-recommended weekend Christian marriage retreat, participating in a couples' support group through your church, or enlisting the help of a licensed Christian marriage counselor.

This is not a hopeless situation. In fact, compared to many marital conflicts, it's a state that can more quickly and remarkably improve—when two children of God who are committed to their marriage decide to work on it and seek appropriate help.

—*Phillip J. Swihart*

TAKING IT PERSONALLY

1. On a scale of one to ten, with ten highest, to what degree do you and your groom (or groom-to-be) fit the "debate vs. relate" pattern? How have differences in your communication styles affected your relationship so far?

2. Try the communication exercise described in this chapter. For ten minutes, tell your partner about feelings or issues you have; he listens, responding only with, "I don't understand; could you restate that?" or "What I hear you saying is . . ." Then he talks for ten minutes and you listen, asking only for clarification or affirmation that you're hearing him accurately. Neither of you is allowed to try to "straighten the other one out," react angrily to something you didn't want to hear, or debate the issue. During the next such "date," your partner will talk first, you second.

Is It Okay to Fight?

23

In a word, no.

That assumes "fighting" isn't just disagreeing and expressing negative emotions. Those things are inevitable in a marriage. But if fighting is trying to resolve those feelings and problems through abusive behavior, it's unhealthy.

Conflict occurs when two people have a difference of opinion that hasn't been resolved. This can happen when you and your spouse disagree over where to go for dinner, whose family to spend the holidays with, or what each person's chores were this week. All of these are normal marital conflicts that can be worked out.

When arguments turn into verbal or physical abuse, though, it isn't healthy for any marriage. If you consistently attack your spouse with statements like, "I'm sorry I married you," "You are so stupid," and "I hate you," you've moved from arguing to abusing.

If you throw things at your spouse—pillows, silverware, pictures, vases—it only leads to more conflict and hurt. And you *never* hit, push, shove, kick, or spit at your spouse. This is physical abuse. Not only is it immoral and illegal, but it causes tremendous damage to your relationship. If this is the way you deal with conflict, you need to seek counseling to learn appropriate ways to reconcile.

Those appropriate ways don't include simply submerging your

differences instead of dealing with them honestly. Many couples try to sidestep or hide their conflict because disagreements can be painful. That leads some spouses to think their own arguments are abnormal.

"I never see other couples fight," Gary told a friend. "It makes me feel like Katie and I have a bad marriage." Gary doesn't realize that some couples share their conflicts openly, while others are more private. Some couples appear to have no conflicts, but in time they often have distress in their marriages because they had just internalized conflict and allowed hurt and resentment to build. Their anger may explode, doing incredible damage to the relationship.

A husband we'll call Paul was one who tried to suppress conflict because he feared fighting. "I fell in love with Lucy because we never fought before we got married," he told his accountability group. "I am so afraid of divorce because of my parents. They fought all the time and look where it led them. If Lucy and I continue to fight, I'm afraid we'll end up like my folks."

Contrary to what Paul believed, divorce is most common when conflict is hidden or unresolved—not when it's dealt with openly. Conflict in itself doesn't lead to divorce. Lack of resolution has brought divorce at worst and unhappy marriages at best.

Conflict resolution may sound complicated, but it's possible. It's a skill that requires the commitment of both spouses and can be refined with practice.

Here are 10 things to remember about resolving conflict without fighting.

1. *Deal with disagreements as soon as possible.* Confront issues as they arise. The longer a conflict stews, the larger the issue becomes;

time tends to magnify a hurt. As the Bible says, "Do not let the sun go down while you are still angry, and do not give the devil a foothold" (Ephesians 4:26).

2. *Be specific.* Communicate clearly what the issue is. Don't generalize with words like "never" or "always." When you're vague, your spouse has to guess what the problem is. Try something like, "It frustrates me when you don't take the trash out on Mondays," rather than, "You never do what you say you're going to do."

3. *Attack the problem, not the person.* Lashing out at your spouse leaves him hurt and defensive. This works against resolving conflict. Your goal is reconciliation and healing in your relationship. Let your mate hear what the problem is from your point of view. Say something like, "I'm frustrated that the bills didn't get paid on time," instead of, "You're so irresponsible and lazy. You never pay anything on time."

4. *Express feelings.* Use "I" statements to share your understanding of the conflict: "I feel hurt when you don't follow through." "It makes me angry when you tease me in front of your friend." Avoid "you" statements like, "You're so insensitive and bossy."

5. *Stick with the subject at hand.* Most people can deal with only one issue at a time. Unfortunately, many spouses bring two or three issues to an argument, trying to reinforce their point. This confuses the confrontation and doesn't allow for understanding and resolution. It's better to say, "It hurt my feelings when you didn't include me in your conversation during dinner with our friends," rather than, "You never include anyone, you always think of yourself. Whenever we're with other people, you always ignore me. Everyone thinks you're selfish."

6. *Confront privately.* Doing so in public could humiliate—or at least embarrass—your spouse. This will immediately put him on the defensive and shut down any desire to reconcile.

7. *Seek to understand the other person's point of view.* Try to put yourself in your spouse's shoes, an exercise that can lead to understanding and restoration. That's what Mia was doing when she told her sister, "Jeff had a hard day at the office today. His boss chewed him out. That's why he's quieter than normal, so I didn't take it personally. I know when I've had a hard day, I need time for myself, too."

8. *Set up a resolution plan.* After the two of you have expressed your points of view and come to an understanding, share your needs and decide where to go from here. That might mean saying something like, "In the future, it would help to discuss with me how we'll spend our savings—rather than telling me after the fact."

9. *Be willing to admit when you're wrong.* Sometimes a conflict occurs because one person's behavior was inappropriate. Be willing to confess and ask forgiveness from your spouse if you've wronged him. That process can help to heal the damage in your relationship. Try something like, "I'm sorry I was unkind to you. Will you please forgive me?" If you're the offended spouse, be gracious enough to accept your spouse's apology.

10. *Remember that maintaining the relationship is more important than winning the argument.* Winning an argument at the expense of losing the relationship is a defeat for both of you. Finding a solution that benefits both spouses lets everybody win.

What if the two of you just can't seem to find that solution? When you can't get past a specific conflict, seek the help of a counselor.

Fighting isn't healthy, but conflict isn't always bad. In fact, it can be a tool for strengthening relationships. When conflict is handled correctly, two people share their hearts with each other, trying to listen and be heard while connecting on a deep level. When you deal with conflict in a caring and positive way, the result can be a deeper relationship and greater intimacy.

"In your anger do not sin" (Ephesians 4:26). God knew that we'd have anger and conflict in our relationships. But anger isn't a sin as long as we seek to resolve the conflict.

"If it is possible, as far as it depends on you, live at peace with everyone" (Romans 12:18). Instead of fighting, are you doing your part to reconcile and restore your relationship with your mate?

—Sheryl DeWitt

TAKING IT PERSONALLY

1. How do you and your groom (or groom-to-be) define "fighting"? How would each of you answer the question, "What was your first fight"?

2. As individuals, make lists of the "10 things to remember about resolving conflict without fighting." But put them in the order reflecting how important you believe they are. Then compare results. Next, give yourselves 10 minutes to reach consensus as a couple on the order of the listed items. Be sure to follow the 10 "rules" as you have your discussion.

How Can We Work Out Disagreements?

24

Whether you've been married five years or engaged for five days, you've had disagreements with your man. *Having* them is not the issue. The real issue is whether you can deal with them in a healthy way. Destructive patterns of disagreement can leave behind emotional scars that never heal.

Most couples think their clashes are unique, but conflict has been around since Adam and Eve. Instead of learning from our ancestors' mistakes, though, we tend to copy them. If Mom screamed and threw CorningWare at Dad when she was angry, daughter will tend to do the same in her own marriage. If Dad withdrew by watching TV every time conflict arose, son will be inclined to follow his example.

No matter what was modeled by your parents, however, you can reframe your thinking. You can realign the way you handle disagreements to better reflect the pattern God wants to see.

Can you imagine Jesus dealing with disagreements as we often do with our spouses? How would He feel about the way you treat your mate during a heated argument?

"But that's just the way I am," you might say. "Besides, my spouse keeps provoking me!" Instead of justifying our behavior, we need to discover how to properly react to disagreements no matter how intense they may be or who's at fault.

Each time you work out a disagreement in a healthy way, you're better equipped to deal with the next one. Conflict handled properly can fine-tune a relationship: "As iron sharpens iron, so one man sharpens another" (Proverbs 27:17).

Resolving disagreements can also "unstick" a couple, moving the two of you to new levels of intimacy and growth. Some of the closest moments a couple can experience often arrive after resolving conflicts. It's like a lightning storm on a warm summer night; though the lightning itself may be scary, it helps to clean the air. Negatively charged ions produced by the storm attach themselves to pollutants, which fall to the ground. That's why the air smells so clean at those times.

The same is true when you deal with disagreements in an appropriate way. Even if the discussion is loud and animated, it can help to rid relationships of contaminants and move you in a positive direction.

To understand how to handle disagreements effectively, let's first look at some techniques that *don't* work.

1. *Denial.* Why are so many married women in our society depressed? Quite a few psychologists believe it's because they don't feel free to discuss frustrations and disagreements with their husbands. That's because husbands tend to deny such problems and refuse to confront them.

Some men simply don't know how to deal with disagreements properly, but many have discovered a payoff in not resolving conflict. They can maintain control by refusing to discuss problems, keeping their wives guessing about the state of their relationship. Wives then hold back because they've discovered that keeping peace with their husbands keeps the men in a good mood and increases the chances of intimacy.

This is not a healthy approach. Failing to resolve disagreements affects our relationships as arthritis does our bodies; it impairs movement, slows us down, and causes a lot of pain. The only way to deal with "relational arthritis" is to develop healthy responses to conflict.

2. *Downplaying.* This is the "Oh, it's nothing" response. This often happens when you feel that dealing with the issue is an exercise in futility. You tell yourself that things will only turn out like before—with your spouse not listening and with both of you upset.

But downplaying the significance of a problem doesn't make it go away. It only sets a negative precedent for dealing with future disagreements.

3. *Exaggeration.* Don't make a disagreement bigger than it is. Not every minor irritation and difference in perspective has to be dissected and "put to rest." Does it really matter if your spouse doesn't share your enthusiasm for sweet pickles and the Three Stooges? Does either of you have to win a debate over which brand of paper towel or route to your church is best?

4. *Nagging.* Don't fall prey to the idea that picking a fight is the best way to get your spouse's attention and deal with a disagreement. Constant nagging is a common example of such erroneous thinking.

A dad was watching the Atlanta Braves on TV one day when his four-year-old came up and wanted to wrestle. Just to see how the boy would respond, the father ignored him and stared at the game. The child made faces, waved, and jumped up and down, but Dad gave no response. Finally the boy knocked on his father's forehead and asked, "Hey, Dad, are you in there?"

Lesson: It's better to do a little gentle "knocking" than to incite a riot to get your mate's attention. "A gentle answer turns away wrath, but a harsh word stirs up anger" (Proverbs 15:1).

5. *Resurrecting the dead.* Bringing up lifeless issues from previous disagreements only "stirs the stink." Perhaps that's why the apostle Paul wrote that love "keeps no record of wrongs" (I Corinthians 13:5).

When a disagreement is over, it's over! Don't rehash old arguments. Some counselors suggest that couples shouldn't bring up an issue that's more than a month or two old. In other words, don't get *historical* in your marriage by continually bringing up the past!

So much for the don'ts. Here are some positive ways to deal with disagreements in your marriage.

1. *Pick the right time and place.* Get away from the telephone, TV, pager, e-mail, and other distractions. Pick a soothing, peaceful environment; a Saturday shopping trip at Sam's Club isn't a good time or place to resolve conflict! Neither are moments when you're going out the door, sitting down to dinner, or lying down for a good night's rest.

Be willing to say, "I agree that this is important, but we need to wait till later to talk about it. Let's go out tomorrow night." Allowing 24 hours to cool down and think is often a wise alternative anyway.

2. *Be prepared.* Understand that emotional events like birthdays, weddings, holidays, anniversaries, and graduations are a natural breeding ground for disagreements. People tend to be "wired and tired"; little sparks can ignite big fires. Try to get plenty of rest before these events, and give your spouse extra grace and forgiveness.

3. *Talk about yourself.* When discussing disagreements, learn to use "I" statements such as "I think" or "I feel"—rather than "you say" or "you always . . ." "You" accusations are usually meant to hurt, not to bring peace and understanding.

4. *Listen more than you talk.* Seek to understand where your partner is coming from, even when you may not agree with his viewpoint. Learn to listen instead of just trying to figure out what you're going to say next.

Temper and control what you think you have a right to say, too. As Ogden Nash put it, "To keep your marriage brimming with love in the loving cup, whenever you're wrong, admit it; whenever you're right, shut up."

5. *Keep your fingers to yourself.* Pointing fingers may be acceptable when correcting toddlers or pets, but it's not healthy between spouses. Pointing is a form of attacking, indicating that the recipient has done something terribly wrong—which often isn't the case. And no one, including your spouse, likes to have a finger wagged in his face.

6. *Keep your arguments out of the bedroom.* That's a place for unity and intimacy, not hashing out differences. Don't use sex (or lack thereof) to manipulate your partner. Sex was never designed to be used as a weapon, withheld without mutual consent (1 Corinthians 7:3-5).

7. *Remember that it's your problem, too.* It's tempting to say, "I don't have the problem, you have the problem!" But if there's trouble in your relationship, it belongs to both of you!

You're a vital part of a *marriage system.* When one part of the system is out of kilter, it throws the entire system off balance. It's like touching a mobile hanging over a baby crib; disturb part of it, and you affect the whole thing.

When you view your spouse's problem as your own, you're much more likely to get serious about helping to work it out. This makes a "double-win"—rather than an "I win, you lose" scenario—more likely.

8. *Learn to see through conflict.* Search for the real issues that often lie beneath the surface. Say, "Wait a minute. We keep arguing about all kinds of irrelevant stuff. What's the *real* problem here?"

9. *Bring God into the conversation.* Ask Him for wisdom when you can't seem to find the answers (James 1:5-6). And if the two of you are Christians, nothing will put a heated argument on "pause" more quickly than two small words: "Let's pray!"

10. *Remember your vows.* Don't threaten divorce during conflict. Threats will only intensify the pain—and leave scars. "For better or worse" will not be stricken from your vows simply because you're in the middle of a major disagreement.

Are you and your spouse disagreeing? Look for mutually beneficial solutions that resolve the tension. If the conflict is too intense to handle, or if one spouse gets extremely emotional, call a time-out until you've both calmed down. If that doesn't help, involve a counselor to assist you in getting perspective.

You can't eliminate disagreements in your relationship. But by taking a proactive approach early in your marriage, you can learn to address conflict in a way that makes everyone—including the Lord—smile.

—Mitch Temple

TAKING IT PERSONALLY

1. How did your parents deal with conflict when you were growing up? How did your mate's parents handle it? How do these models compare with the way you'd like to handle it in your marriage?

2. Which of this chapter's five "techniques that don't work" have the two of you tried? What happened? Which of the ten positive suggestions will you put into practice next time you face a disagreement? What's a signal (for example, pointing to your eyes to symbolize "Learn to see through conflict") that will help remind you to do that?

Do I Have to Forgive My Husband?

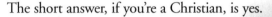

25

The short answer, if you're a Christian, is yes.

Jesus Christ has been crystal clear on that subject: "And when you stand praying, if you hold anything against anyone, forgive him, so that your Father in heaven may forgive you your sins" (Mark 11:25).

The apostle Paul echoes this idea: "Bear with each other and forgive whatever grievances you may have against one another. Forgive as the Lord forgave you" (Colossians 3:13).

Short answers to profound questions, however, are not always completely satisfying. On the surface, they seem to gloss over the complexities.

After all, some offenses are so grievous that it's difficult to *want* to forgive a person who's betrayed your trust and his vows to God—much less actually *do* so. Putting things in perspective, of course, most offenses in marriage don't rise to that level of pain and destructiveness.

Both Jesus and Paul answered this question by emphasizing that the most important reason to forgive is that we've been forgiven. If we've asked for God's forgiveness through Jesus' sacrifice, for our terribly long list of offenses against Him (and if we think we haven't offended Him, we're really out of touch with reality), He's already forgiven us. Why would we do less for those—including our spouses—who have wronged us?

Another good reason for forgiving a spouse is that it's in your own best interest to do so. As in art, what isn't positive space is negative space. What's left if we decide not to take the positive step of forgiving? The negatives of depression, anger, self-pity, and bitterness will be fertilized.

Not to forgive is costly—to the person who chooses not to do so, and to those around that person—even more than to the target of the person's chronic wrath.

Some husbands and wives seem highly invested in keeping minutes of all past sins and offenses of their spouses. *Ka-ching, ka-ching, ka-ching*—the cash register of marital history just keeps adding up the injustices, great and small, perceived and real.

One day that gunnysack of unforgiven hurts becomes so heavy that the aggrieved spouse, irritated by some insignificant infraction, feels the irresistible urge to dump them on the other's head. The pent-up poison of accrued bitterness blows out like a volcanic eruption. The recipient feels righteously indignant that a major injustice, a massive overreaction to nothing, has been perpetrated on him or her. This exchange, born of many choices not to forgive, solves nothing, resolves nothing, heals nothing.

Failing to forgive also gets a relationship stuck in an unending, repetitive cycle of blaming each other—rather than taking responsibility for one's shortcomings. This is a no-growth, slow-death strategy, again filling what could be positive space with negative space, which can doom marriages. It's also a terrible model for children to follow and to pass on to future generations.

But what about offenses that seem almost unforgivable? What about a father who sexually abuses his children, or an unrepentant wife who flaunts a lesbian affair? How do you forgive that?

Ultimately, forgiveness is an attitude—one that may be understood only by you and the Lord. It's giving up your insistence on getting revenge. It is not sweeping a crime under the rug or denying the enormity of what an offender has done.

In the case of abuse, your first action may need to be ensuring your safety and that of your children, if any. Forgiving a violent or perverted spouse is not the same as being naïve or stupid about his or her potential to do further harm.

Forgiveness is also not equivalent to forgetting a spouse's track record. It doesn't mean that an abusive husband or wife will be immediately allowed back into the family home after a quick, superficial, even tearful "repentance." It doesn't mean that an unfaithful spouse must be welcomed back without a commitment to counseling and behavior change.

There are times, for example, when a wife is afraid to forgive her serially adulterous husband for fear that he'll only betray and hurt her again. Her instincts may be exactly right; he'll be chasing another skirt within a month. Forgiving him does not mean that she must permit him to continue his sinful lifestyle and remain in a sham marriage to her.

One husband, Brent, began "staying late for work." His wife, Shannon, happened on a cell phone bill that included many calls to one number she didn't recognize. Some of these calls were made late at night and on weekends. When she called the number, a woman who turned out to work in Brent's office answered.

This all seemed heartbreakingly familiar to Shannon. Brent had been involved in two affairs—that she knew of—during their marriage. This was number three. The old feelings of hurt, betrayal, and anger came flooding back.

In the past, Brent had been very "repentant" when caught. She thought she'd forgiven him. Now she wasn't so sure. The only certain thing was that she wasn't about to forgive him again; she'd had it.

If you're at the edge of this cliff, married to an abusive spouse or a mate who's continued to trash you and your marriage vows through sexual infidelity, seek the help of a pastor or Christian marriage counselor.

If the situation isn't that grave, but you harbor an unforgiving spirit and find it impossible to let go, ask God to give you the power to *want* to forgive. Then commit yourself to doing so.

"But what good will that do?" you might ask.

First, it will restore your fellowship with God that may have been quenched due to this issue in your spiritual life.

Second, it will open the door—at least in relationships that haven't been irretrievably damaged—to the possibility of healing and restoration with your spouse. It may bring greater intimacy than you've had in a long time.

Finally, it can bring freedom from the bonds of resentment, allowing emotional health—perhaps even better physical health. It can build a greater sense of joy and peace to fill that negative space in your life—and displace the occupant of bitterness.

—*Phillip J. Swihart*

TAKING IT PERSONALLY

1. How often do you tend to empty the "gunnysack of grievances" you have against your groom (or groom-to-be)? Would you
recommend this approach
to other brides? Why or
why not?

2. If you struggle to forgive
something your partner has done, is
it time to talk with a pastor or counselor
about the situation? What do you think will
happen if you don't? If you fear that forgiving
your partner will only encourage him to continue hurting you, how
could a counselor help to keep that from happening?

How Can I Get Him to Forgive Me?

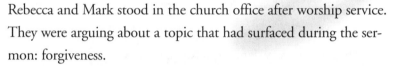

26

Rebecca and Mark stood in the church office after worship service. They were arguing about a topic that had surfaced during the sermon: forgiveness.

Mark couldn't seem to refrain from bringing Rebecca's mistake up again. Nine months ago, while Mark had been away on an extended business trip, she'd contacted an old boyfriend simply because she was lonely and curious about what he was doing these days.

Nothing else had occurred between the two. But when Mark had found the guy's number on her cell phone bill, he'd imagined the worst.

Rebecca had been penitent and tearful. She'd realized it was inappropriate and had asked Mark more than once to forgive her. But he seemed unable to do that.

Now they stood in the church office, clashing again over the incident. Almost everyone had gone home after the service.

James, an older deacon, could tell the young couple was having a fight as he walked by the office's glass door. After several moments he approached the pair and asked whether they were okay.

They said they were, but admitted something had come up

during the sermon that exposed old wounds. James figured it was connected with forgiveness.

"You know," he said, "when my wife and I were first married, I did something stupid which I regretted a long time. And though she is now gone on, she did something that I will never forget. She taught me a lot."

He gently placed his hand on Mark's shoulder. "If I can help you," James added with tenderness, "let me know. I will be praying for you." Then he walked away.

Curiosity got the best of the couple. That evening, Mark called James and asked if he and Rebecca could drop by Tuesday evening to hear the rest of the story. James quickly agreed.

After Mark and Rebecca arrived at the little house, James asked them to tell him a little about their problem. After several minutes of listening, he began to relate his own story.

While serving in the Korean conflict, James had been unfaithful to his wife. Overcome with shame, he'd confessed his sin to her the evening he returned from duty.

For the next several months, James worked to earn back his wife's trust. After proving his love through many difficult days, he received a special gift from her.

Now James pulled a piece of yellowed paper from his Bible and handed it to Mark. On it was the following:

"Let all bitterness, and wrath, and anger, and clamor, and evil speaking, be put away from you, with all malice: And be ye kind one to another, tenderhearted, forgiving one another, even as God for Christ's sake hath forgiven you" (Ephesians 4:31-32, KJV).

Under the Scripture passage was written the following: "James, I forgive you. If I were in your shoes, I may have done the same thing.

God burned this verse on my heart and I have obeyed. You have proven yourself worthy of forgiveness and through the months I have learned how to forgive you. I love you and believe in you. Forever yours, Sue."

James wiped one lonesome tear from his eye. "The gift she gave me was forgiveness," he said. "I hope you two will learn to forgive each other like my wife did for me."

That night changed Mark and Rebecca forever. Though they both came from homes where forgiveness was sparse, they committed to learn how to forgive and be forgiven.

Like Mark and Rebecca, most couples struggle with learning how to forgive. It's not something that comes naturally for us; it's something we learn to do. Jesus must have known that when He commanded us to pray for our enemies. He knew it wouldn't happen by itself, but that a directive was needed.

Is your spouse having a hard time forgiving you? There are some things you can do to help.

1. *Recognize that forgiveness is a process.* It ebbs and flows; it starts, stops, and starts again; it gets better and gets worse. No matter what the issue is that caused your spouse to be hurt, forgiveness can be more than just a one-shot decision. Understand that forgiving you may take time.

If your mate occasionally seems to struggle with or dwell on what you did, that doesn't necessarily equal a refusal to forgive. Sights, sounds, and memories can trigger an episode of struggle. If you're impatient or inconsiderate, it will only cause more hurt. Pursue understanding, not just the desire to put the conflict behind you.

2. *Realize that fear can be a barrier to forgiveness.* Fear often blocks mercy. Here are three kinds of fear that can delay the process:

- *Fear of losing control or power.* To help your mate let go of his need to control the situation, demonstrate your trustworthiness and show that you understand the seriousness of what you've done. Let your spouse see that you have to live with the consequences every day; assure him regularly that you've learned a great deal about how deeply your actions have affected him. Show how you're taking steps to prevent the mistake from occurring again.

- *Fear of not being able to punish the wrongdoing.* Maybe your spouse is still in the anger stage and wants you to experience some of the hurt he felt. Be patient during this stage of the process, whether your mate is right or wrong. Pray for your spouse; ask God to reveal your broken heart and your desire to make things right. Eventually your spouse may start asking himself, *Why can't I forgive? What payoff am I getting out of not forgiving?* Questions like these often lead to healing, but it takes time.

- *Fear of forgetting what occurred.* Help your spouse realize that you don't expect him to not remember what happened. That's impossible. Explain that you simply look forward to the day when he will be affected less by your actions, and to the opportunity of proving your commitment to make your marriage healthy again. Be as understanding as possible. Impatience will only underline the suspicion that you don't care what your partner is struggling with.

3. *Seek outside guidance.* If necessary, ask a professional counselor or older Christian to help you and your spouse with the process. You might be surprised to know how many people you respect have struggled with and triumphed over issues of forgiveness. Make sure, though, that your spouse is open to this help. An outsider may be

perceived as a threat or as an additional source of embarrassment.

4. *Be honest with yourself.* It's easy to see your spouse's failure to forgive when you're confident that your heart is genuinely remorseful. But keep checking your own attitude and actions during your journey to forgiveness. Ask the following questions:

- *What exactly caused my spouse to be hurt?* It's easy to forget what the real issue is and focus on distractions.
- *What behaviors or attitudes do I hold on to that cause more hurt?*
- *What's my plan to make necessary changes?*
- *What might God be showing me in my spouse's inability to forgive?*
                                                              —Mitch Temple

Taking It Personally

1. If your spouse were to write you a letter of forgiveness as James' wife did, what do you wish it would say?

2. What's one thing you can do this week to apply each of the following recommendations? (a) Demonstrate your trustworthiness; (b) show that you understand the seriousness of what you've done; (c) let your spouse see that you have to live with the consequences every day; (d) assure him regularly that you've learned a great deal about how deeply your actions have affected him; (e) show how you're taking steps to prevent the mistake from occurring again.

How Can Faith Keep
Us Together?

27

Every marriage needs a bond to sustain it during the trials that will surface. Is faith in Christ really the glue that can keep a marriage together?

After all, some statistics seem to indicate that evangelicals divorce at a higher rate than those with no connection to religion. As Glenn Stanton, director of social research and cultural affairs and senior analyst for marriage and sexuality at Focus on the Family writes, "We often hear that divorce rates among people who identified themselves with certain denominations and lived in the Southern Bible Belt states had higher divorce rates than people with no religious affiliation. . . . [But] religious commitment, rather than mere religious affiliation, contributes to greater levels of marital success."[1]

Stanton notes that sociologists David Popenoe and Scott Stanley explain that the "Bible Belt" statistics result mainly from higher poverty rates and marriage at younger ages—not religious participation. In fact, University of Virginia sociologist Brad Wilcox found that evangelicals who attend church regularly have a divorce rate 35 percent lower than secular couples, after adjusting for factors like economic and educational status.[2]

But how does faith make a difference?

When Kay and Carl married, they made a commitment to honor each other. They hoped nothing could break their bond. They had high moral values and a personal relationship with the Lord. Their security was in Jesus—not in themselves, not in each other.

They were beginning in the right direction. Could they stay the course?

It didn't take Kay long to realize that Carl had a lot of faults she'd failed to recognize. One was his inept handling of their money.

Kay had a choice. She could handle the problem in a way that was consistent with her faith, which took the authority of the Bible seriously. Or she could turn elsewhere for advice.

She decided to take an approach that echoed 1 Peter 3:3-6: "Your beauty . . . should be that of your inner self, the unfading beauty of a gentle and quiet spirit, which is of great worth in God's sight. For this is the way the holy women of the past who put their hope in God used to make themselves beautiful. They were submissive to their own husbands, like Sarah, who obeyed Abraham and called him her master. You are her daughters if you do what is right and do not give way to fear."

When Kay respectfully and graciously confronted Carl with their dilemma, he was able to hear her instead of being defensive. Now it was his turn to decide whether his response would reflect his faith.

He decided to apply principles he'd learned in 1 Timothy 3:3-6, especially the instructions to be gentle, not quarrelsome or proud or greedy. In particular, he didn't allow pride to get in the way of learning new budgeting methods.

In other words, faith helped keep them together.

Kay and Carl faced another challenge when it came to in-laws.

Carl's mother had never really been excited about her only son marrying anyone—including Kay. Every family gathering was uncomfortable for Kay, and she began to feel resentful. She wanted to yell at Carl and tell him to defend her.

Instead, she prayed about the problem. She asked God to make it clear to Carl what his role as a husband should be in this situation.

Before long, Carl was choosing to follow 1 Corinthians 16:13-14: "Be on your guard; stand firm in the faith; be men of courage; be strong. Do everything in love." He took a more active part in supporting his wife, and did it in a loving way. Once again, faith helped keep these spouses together.

Then came another challenge. Carl and Kay moved to another state, leaving the church that had been an awesome support system for them. Knowing what a difference faith had made to them individually and as a couple, they looked in their new location for the nurturing and fellowship of other believers. They found it in a church with solid teaching, where they began to volunteer. Again their faith provided resources that strengthened their relationship.

Faith helps keep couples together despite the smaller challenges of everyday life, too. When Carl offends Kay, for example, her understanding of what the Bible says about forgiveness is activated. So is her commitment to apply those principles. She knows that God has graciously extended forgiveness to her, and expects her to do the same for others (Matthew 18:23-35). This helps her to have a forgiving heart toward Carl, preventing a root of bitterness—a marriage killer—from taking hold. Forgiveness is a vital ingredient of the glue that holds marriages together.

So is fidelity. Carl and Kay have pledged to be faithful to one another, which might prove difficult for Carl in his job. He works with women who are congenial and attractive. All the temptations are there—travel, creative teamwork, the opportunity to share confidences. Carl isn't blind, but the eyes of his heart are enlightened (Ephesians 1:18). Having received the gift of a relationship with God, he's not about to mess it up. He chooses to "avoid every kind of evil" (1 Thessalonians 5:22). His commitment to Kay flows from his commitment to the Lord.

If you're a follower of Christ, staying together as a couple involves the same things that living your faith does—constantly putting aside pride, working daily on fully accepting God's forgiveness, and seeking to do what pleases Him. The following passage applies to marriage as it does to all of life: "Therefore, since we are surrounded by such a great cloud of witnesses, let us throw off everything that hinders and the sin that so easily entangles, and let us run with perseverance the race marked out for us" (Hebrews 12:1).

Can faith keep you together? God's Word says it can.

—*Betty Jordan*

Taking It Personally

1. What role has faith played in your relationship with your groom (or groom-to-be) so far? If it hasn't played an important role, should you count on it to keep your marriage together?

2. Which of the following are you will-
ing to do this month in order to build up your supply of "faith-based relationship glue"? (a) Join a small group Bible study; (b) pray regularly with your mate; (c) take turns reading from a book about spiritual growth; (d) work together in a church service project.

WHAT IF AN IN-LAW
DOESN'T ACCEPT ME?

28

Heather and Steve have been married almost four years. They love each other very much, but relationships with their in-laws have always been strained.

Heather feels Steve's mother is overly critical of how Heather parents the children. She also gets upset over her mother-in-law's statements about how Steve works much too hard; she sees them as attacks on her choice to be a stay-at-home mom.

Steve has great difficulty connecting with his father in-law, who seems to live for sports. When Steve and Heather visit his in-laws, Steve is especially disturbed to see Heather share her father's sports mania—leaving Steve feeling like an outsider.

It's normal to want to be accepted by your in-laws. But feeling that you *need* to be accepted can bring complications, causing you to be uncomfortable and unnatural around them.

Unrealistic hopes cause problems, too. Many parents are initially over-protective of their own child, or have expectations that no spouse can meet in the beginning.

Often new husbands and wives assume they'll be loved and accepted by in-laws on the merit of having married the in-laws' child. This may be the case, but it usually takes time to establish trust and respect. Just as it takes time to build other close relationships, gaining acceptance into a family doesn't happen instantly.

After all, you're stepping into a family with a long history of established bonds. Don't be too hard on yourself and expect too much. If your relationship with your own parents is wonderful, the one with your mother- and father-in-law may never measure up. If your relationship with your parents isn't good, you may be too needy and demanding in trying to make up for it.

The number-one factor in resolving problems of acceptance by in-laws is your spouse's support. As with all close relationships, it's an art to support your spouse without jumping into the fight or feeding his or her discontent.

Let's say that Heather and Steve have just returned from an extended visit with his parents. She declares: "I never want to stay with your parents again! Why doesn't your mother like me? She told me that she had you potty trained by age two and that you obeyed her without question."

In this case, Heather is being a little overdramatic and overly sensitive. How can Steve support her without reinforcing her exaggeration or condemning his mom?

He could say something like this: "Honey, I'm so sorry that you feel hurt by the things my mom says. But I know you're a terrific mother, and she'll come to see that, too. She also seems to remember me as much more perfect than I was. I can remember plenty of frustration and grief, but it's probably good that she doesn't remember all the tough times. I'll always support you in finding a time to share your feelings with my mom. I really think she likes you and can't help but love you as time goes on."

Or imagine that Ken has the complaint. "I don't want to spend more than one day at your parents' house ever again," he says. "I always feel like a third wheel. I know your dad hates the fact that I don't enjoy sports. You and he seem to be in your own little 'sports world.' What am I supposed to do, spend my time helping your mom in the kitchen?"

Heather might respond by reassuring Ken along these lines: "I'm so sorry that I haven't been more sensitive to your feelings of being left out during those times. You're right—sports has been the major thing Dad and I share. I know even Mom has felt a little left out when we obsess about it. Let's see if we can think of ways to connect when we're at my parents—all of us, including my mom. I know my dad primarily cares how I'm loved and taken care of, and there's no question about those things in my mind. Please give me a little sign if I forget it next time."

When it comes to dealing with an in-law who doesn't seem to accept you, here are the main principles to remember:

- Learn to support your spouse without getting hooked into taking sides.
- Encourage your spouse to share his feelings directly with you.
- Keep a sense of humor.
- Show your spouse that he is number one in your eyes.
- Don't take things too personally.
- Remember, building a relationship takes time.
- Forgive, forgive, forgive.
- Remember that you're loving your spouse by honoring his parents.

One more idea: When confronted with what feels like a no-win situation involving an in-law, use the "drop the rope" theory. Imagine a rope, the kind used in a tug-of-war. If you find yourself provoked, see that rope in your hands. You can choose to continue yanking on it—or drop it. Dropping it may sound as though you're giving in or giving up, but it's actually very empowering. It's also much more effective than tugging back and forth.

For Ken and Heather, a solution may look something like this:

- They discuss the things their in-laws say and do that tend to trigger anxiety and anger.
- They agree to act as "buffers" for each other against possible hard spots.
- They commit to forgiving any offense quickly.
- They plan to give the relationships time to develop.
- They start working as a team.
- They can even see some humor in learning to drop those "invisible ropes."

As a result, each of them feels more loved and supported. That helps them enjoy getting to know and appreciate each other's parents.

—Romie Hurley

TAKING IT PERSONALLY

1. When was the last time that "dropping the rope" might have helped you get along with your in-laws? What did you do instead?

2. If your spouse (or spouse-to-be) could grant you three wishes concerning acceptance from your in-laws, what would they be? How could your mate make the situation less stressful for you (discuss your feelings, act as a buffer, work as a team, point out your good qualities to his parents, etc.)? Try requesting that help this week.

How Can We Keep from Drifting Apart?

29

"We just drifted apart."

So many couples cite this as the reason for their divorce that you might think it's inevitable. Is it? If not, how can you prevent it?

Robin admits that she and her husband, Tony, are drifting apart. "We have different interests now. He's immersed in his work, and I'm at home all day with our three sons. I gave up my career to raise a family while Tony gets promotions. When Tony gets home, he has nothing left for me. He doesn't really love me."

Many couples seem to feel marriage is like selecting the right plane—and then putting it on autopilot. That's a good way to ensure that spouses eventually drift apart.

Here's how it often works: One partner is satisfied with the relationship as it is, but the other's needs are overlooked. In the case of Robin and Tony, Tony has been the mostly happy one. He has a beautiful wife, three great kids, a relationship with the Lord, and a job he enjoys. He's seen himself as having made the right choices—so from now on, it's smooth sailing. Autopilot has seemed to work for him.

Robin, on the other hand, is wondering whether she made the

right choice of "plane." She needs more of Tony's presence to feel valued.

In a bid for Tony's attention, Robin has started distancing herself from him. His reaction is to feel inadequate, disappointed in himself that he can't make his wife happy, unworthy of her love, and confused. He's thinking, *What am I doing wrong?*

Instead of disclosing her needs, Robin is expecting Tony to do some mindreading. When he fails, she withdraws her love. He, in turn, feels rejected and helpless to please her. Closeness evaporates, replaced by confusion and disappointment.

The result: Their relationship feels empty. They're drifting apart.

Robin and Tony need to understand that marriage is a growing, living relationship that needs nurturing. Before nurturing can be accepted, though, both partners have to be willing to take responsibility for their feelings and behaviors.

Using "straight talk" to acknowledge emotions without blaming can lead to resolving conflict. Robin could start the process by saying something like, "Tony, when I've had little adult conversation all day, I really need to talk with you."

Is this statement blaming? No. Is it clear what she needs? Yes. This will prevent defensiveness, contempt, and withdrawal.

Robin also can set the stage for solving the problem by putting the kids on a schedule that allows her "alone time" with Tony. The degree of closeness in a marriage reflects the overall climate in a home, and "climate control" takes spending time together.

Robin needs to know how to handle her resentment, too. When thoughts like *He doesn't really love me* arise, what should she do?

When such a thought strolls into the entryway of her mind, it doesn't belong to her yet; she doesn't have to feel guilty about it. But when she "camps on" this resentful thought instead of analyzing and rejecting it, it takes on a life of its own. She accepts ownership and buys into deception. She allows the thought to keep her from respectfully telling Tony what she's experiencing.

There's hope for Robin and Tony. They're both Christians who take their relationship with God seriously, and have been asking Him what to do about drifting apart. With His leading, they're working on making changes like these:

- becoming better listeners;
- taking responsibility for their actions and feelings;
- avoiding blaming;
- being more affectionate and considerate;
- becoming partners in parenting;
- respecting each other's differences;
- supporting each other in extended family conflicts;
- praying individually and as a couple;
- journaling their feelings individually to their heavenly Father;
- placing a priority on time together;
- submitting to God as their authority;
- being proactive by creating a plan.

There are as many reasons for drifting apart as there are marriages. But the way to prevent that drift begins with a single step: taking yourself off autopilot.

—Betty Jordan

TAKING IT PERSONALLY

1. Are you more like Tony or
   Robin? Does taking your
   relationship off autopilot
   sound dangerous, freeing,
   pointless, tiring, or exciting?

2. If you find yourself thinking, *He doesn't
   love me* this week, what will you do? How
   will you avoid "camping on" that thought? How will you analyze
   and reject it? How will you respectfully tell your partner about
   your feelings?

How Can We Keep the Romance Alive?

30

Romance has been described as "idealized love."

Does that mean it's only an infatuation between high school sweethearts? Is it a short-lived attachment? Is it even *meant* to last?

Megan says she and her husband, Terry, have lost the romance in their marriage. They have two children, and Megan spends every waking hour caring for the needs of her family. At the end of the day she's exhausted, with no energy for candlelight dinners.

What should Megan and Terry do? Is there a list of "rules for romance" they need to follow?

Not exactly. It's actually a deeper issue; the presence of romance reflects the overall quality of a maturing relationship.

A man who was one of four sons tells how, every night, his father would come home and walk right past his boys. He would go directly to his wife and give her a hug and a kiss. Then he would turn to the four little stairsteps who were watching, and say, "I think I am falling in love with your mom."

That man—and his sons—knew something about how romance can survive in a marriage.

So what can you do to help romance survive in yours?

1. *Recall your beginnings.* Remember when you first met and fell in love. What characterized your relationship? Did you listen to every word your intended said?

You probably were considerate and filled with respect. Each of you gave the other your complete, constant attention. You overlooked each other's faults and wanted to be together.

Was your love based on reality? Not the "reality" of annoying habits and thoughtless slights you may have catalogued since the honeymoon. But aren't the qualities that attracted you to each other just as real? Maybe it's time to rediscover them.

2. *Give up the spotlight.* Now that Megan and Terry have children, Megan can't give all her attention to Terry. Terry can't do that for Megan, either; he may be focusing on his work or a home project to make life better for his family.

Part of maturity is not needing to be the center of attention. Both Megan and Terry can demonstrate love for each other, but in new ways—indirectly as well as directly. As long as each of them views the other's role with respect and consideration, romance— idealized love—doesn't have to elude them.

3. *Live under God's authority.* Keeping romance alive is a lot easier when you're growing the fruit of the Spirit—love, joy, peace, patience, kindness, goodness (love in action), faithfulness, gentleness, and self-control (Galatians 5:22-23). When Megan and Terry submit to God, the spark of romance not only has a chance of being rekindled, but can become a radiant flame.

4. *Honor each other.* Romance certainly involves emotion. But it's also about valuing our spouses.

When Terry and Megan got married, they both felt love for one another. But when Megan was pregnant, she began to feel neglected by Terry, and a wound was opened. Terry sensed the distancing, and soon he felt unappreciated, too.

Gary and Norma Smalley offer this advice on honoring your spouse: "When you honor your wife, she will sense that nothing and no one in the world is more important to you. She won't have to wonder if she's number one—she'll know."[1] The same goes for a wife's treatment of her husband.

5. *Be honest.* Feeling guilty, Terry and Megan didn't tell each other about their resentment. This could be the beginning of a downward spiral if they don't start opening up. Resentment is an enemy of romance.

If you and your mate feel you can't be honest with each other, let a Christian counselor or pastor help get the conversation going.

Keeping romance alive requires effort and creativity. It means honoring one another by being honest, kind, and respectful in your responses, showing affection throughout the day without expecting sexual intimacy, having a regular date night, lighting candles or having a sweet fragrance in the bedroom, praying together, sharing feelings, and taking responsibility for your offenses. When these are standard operating procedure in Megan and Terry's home—or yours—romance won't be a thing of the past.

Romance is a living, growing love. Things that grow require "tending to." No one can do this alone. It takes both marriage partners giving their all; it takes reliance on the Holy Spirit to empower you, especially in the darkest hours.

God designed romance to be an ever-changing treasure. As your marriage progresses, will you allow the rosebud of romance to mature into full bloom?

—Betty Jordan

Taking It Personally

1. What's the most romantic thing your groom (or groom-to-be) ever did for you? What's the most romantic thing you ever did for him?

2. What do you think romance could look like for the two of you five years from now? Fifteen? Fifty? As a couple, describe a "perfectly romantic evening" you'd like to have on your first wedding anniversary. Write down the description, save it in a "time capsule," and make plans to celebrate that anniversary in a way that reflects what you've written.

Suggested Resources

There are many helpful books and other resources to guide you through the early years of marriage. Check your local bookstore for the following:

Boundaries in Marriage by Dr. Henry Cloud and Dr. John Townsend (Zondervan, 2002)

The DNA of Relationships by Gary Smalley (Tyndale House Publishers, 2004)

For Women Only by Shaunti Feldhahn (Multnomah, 2004)

The Gift of Sex: A Guide to Sexual Fulfillment by Clifford L. Penner and Joyce J. Penner (W Publishing Group, 2003)

Great Expectations: An Interactive Guide to Your First Year of Marriage by Toben and Joanne Heim (NavPress, 2000)

Healing the Hurt in Your Marriage by Dr. Gary and Barbara Rosberg (Focus on the Family/Tyndale House Publishers, 2004)

Hedges: Loving Your Marriage Enough to Protect It by Jerry B. Jenkins (Crossway Books, 2005)

Hidden Keys of a Loving, Lasting Marriage by Gary Smalley and Norma Smalley (Zondervan, 1993)

His Needs, Her Needs: Building an Affair-Proof Marriage by Willard F. Harley, Jr. (Monarch Books, 1994)

How Do You Say, "I Love You"? by Judson Swihart (InterVarsity Press, 1977)

The Language of Love by Gary Smalley and John Trent, Ph.D. (Focus on the Family/Tyndale House Publishing, 2006)

Love and Respect by Dr. Emerson Eggerichs (Integrity Publishers, 2004)

Love for a Lifetime by Dr. James Dobson (Multnomah, 2004)

Love Must Be Tough: New Hope for Families in Crisis by Dr. James Dobson (Multnomah, 2004)

The Most Important Year in a Woman's Life/The Most Important Year in a Man's Life by Robert Wolgemuth, Bobbie Wolgemuth, Mark DeVries, and Susan DeVries (Zondervan, 2003)

Sacred Marriage by Gary Thomas (Zondervan, 2002)

Saving Your Marriage Before It Starts by Les and Leslie Parrott (Zondervan, 1995)

Surviving a Spiritual Mismatch in Marriage by Lee and Leslie Strobel (Zondervan, 2002)

Your Marriage Masterpiece by Al Janssen (Focus on the Family/Tyndale House Publishing, 2008)

The following booklets and recordings are available from Focus on the Family (call 1-800-A-FAMILY):

Accepting Your Mate's Differences by Dr. Kevin Leman (Focus on the Family broadcast CD192)

Building a Marriage That Lasts by Dr. James Dobson (Focus on the Family booklet LF154)

Learning to Communicate by Gary Smalley and John Trent (Focus on the Family broadcast CD111)

Nothing to Hide by Joann Condie (Focus on the Family booklet F00038T)

Notes

How Can Faith Keep Us Together?

1. Glenn Stanton, "The Role Faith Plays in Marriage and the Likelihood of Divorce," (Focus on Social Issues, July 8, 2005), found at http://family.org/cforum/fosi/marriage/divorce/a0037068.cfm.
2. W. Bradford Wilcox, "The Cultural Contradictions of Mainline Family Ideology and Practice," publication pending.

How Can We Keep Romance Alive?

1. Gary and Norma Smalley, *It Takes Two to Tango* (Colorado Springs: Focus on the Family, 1997), p. 25.

Make the most of your relationships with resources from Focus on the Family®!

From dating and engagement to the wedding and beyond, we're here to help your marriage thrive.

First Comes Love, Then What?
Myths about finding Mr. or Mrs. Right are held to be true by too many men and women searching for that one-in-a-million match. It's time for a reality check. Filled with real-life examples and solid principles, this book will help both men and women learn to use their heads before losing their hearts.
Paperback F00727B

Countdown for Couples
Research and common sense indicate that engaged couples will have stronger, more successful marriages if they participate in premarital counseling. Yet with all the planning that goes into a wedding, this important preparation can often be overlooked. *Countdown for Couples* delivers insight in an easy-to-use format and tackles important questions such as: *Are you ready for a lifelong commitment? What should you expect?* And more!
Paperback F00863B

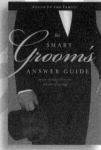

The Savvy Bride's Answer Guide
Your maid of honor might not tell you, but the price of your wedding dress isn't the only thing that may shock you about wedded bliss. During the first year of marriage, you're likely to face all kinds of surprises—from your in-laws' strange traditions to your groom's annoying tendencies. This friendly resource will smooth the road whether you've been engaged for 10 minutes or married for 10 months.
Paperback F00857B

The Smart Groom's Answer Guide
Launching your lifetime love? Getting biblical answers is the smart thing to do! This book provides down-to-earth advice from a team of professional Focus on the Family counselors. You'll get the real story on questions like *What does it mean to be a husband? Why does she want to talk all the time?* And more! Ask now—or forever hold your peace!
Paperback F00856B